GREENWOOD
G U I D E S

The Team

Simon Greenwood

Adam Barnes

Rachel Parsons

Oliver Needham

First published in 2001 by Greenwood Guides,
46 Lillie Rd, London SW6 1TN, UK.

Second edition

Copyright (c) January 2004 Greenwood Guides

All rights reserved. No part of this publication may be reproduced, or transmitted in
any form or by any means, electronically or mechanically, including photocopying,
recording or any information storage or retrieval system without prior written
permission from the publisher. This publication is not included under licences issued
by the Copyright Agency. No part of this publication may be used in any form of
advertising, sales promotion or publicity.

Simon Greenwood has asserted his right to be identified as the author of this work.

ISBN 0-9537980-4-6 printed in China.

THE GREENWOOD GUIDE TO
AUSTRALIA

special hand-picked accommodation

second edition, 2004/5

www.greenwoodguides.com

Acknowledgements

Series Editor Simon Greenwood

Australia Editor Adam Barnes

Writing collaboration and inspections Simon Greenwood, Adam Barnes, Oliver Needham, Rachel Parsons

Cover artwork Patricia Fraser

Design Tory Gordon-Harris

Maps supplied by CollinsBartholomew a subsidiary of HarperCollins*Publishers* Ltd. Reproduced by Permission of HarperCollins Publishers.

Production Jo Ekin

Printing Colorcraft, Hong Kong

UK distribution Portfolio, London

New Zealand distribution Nationwide, Christchurch

Australia distribution Peribo, Sydney

USA and Canada distribution Cimino Publishing Group, New Jersey

Incidental photographs:
Title page: Millhouse on the Bridge, Tasmania, page 95
Queensland, Victoria, Northern Territory by Peter Bray
New South Wales: The Priory at Bingie, page 57
South Australia: Portee Station, page 102
Tasmania, Western Australia by Oliver Needham

Contents

	Map	Page

Symbols
and what they mean

 No credit cards accepted

 Meals can be provided, often by prior arrangement

 Rooms all have TVs

 Children are welcome without proviso

 Working farm

 Off-street car parking

 Access only for wheelchairs

 Full wheelchair facilities

 Swimming available in pool, sea, dam or river

 Good hiking or walking direct from the house

They have their own horses for riding

No smoking inside the buildings

Introduction

Most places to stay do exactly what it says on the tin, BB&B: bed, breakfast and bill. As a result many people think of where they stay as incidental to their holiday, a convenient stopover between things they want to see.

Our approach is quite the opposite. We have found you places where the stay itself IS the holiday. Far more than just the skeleton of your trip, the places we have chosen will put the flesh on it, clothe it, put a hat on its head, wrap a scarf round its neck and pop a pipe in its mouth. We have sought accommodation that acts as destination. The owners in this guide will make sure that you experience the farm, the winery, the rainforest, the bush, the outback, the beach, the reef, the city, the wildlife… don't you worry. But you will also meet extremely hospitable Australians and go places other tourists will not.

I think that of all the accommodation guides I have been involved in, this one to Australia is the most essential for those travellers looking to get a little beneath the surface of the country they are visiting. Many have flown a very long way to get to the country in the first place. They often intend that it should be the one trip of their lifetime there. And they feel duty-bound to tick off the few high-profile icons by which Australian tourism has defined itself: Uluru (Ayers Rock), the Sydney Opera House and Harbour Bridge, the Great Barrier Reef, the Twelve Apostles… even the Blue Mountains and the Hunter, Barossa and Margaret River wine areas. But Australia is just too big to tick off all these places and also leave time for pottering about on country lanes. My advice is, narrow down your ambitions substantially and leave time to explore.

Australia is a revelation. The sun always seems to be shining, Aussies always seem to be outside doing things (annoyingly well)… even cricket matches look like fun in Australia. Away from the obvious places, hardly any of the country seems to be visited by overseas (or indeed any) tourists and I was always happy trundling down dirt tracks towards a farm homestead. I knew I'd see something extraordinary en route: a giant goanna, a flock of cockatoos or parrots, a basking lizard, kangaroos…. So often farmstays or lodges or B&Bs had access to stupendous views or countryside completely unknown by the world at large.

It's not all easy though. We, the Greenwood Guides, have had to work hard. The size of Australia (big) and the distance between towns (big) have, in my view, hindered a crescendo of exciting places to stay goading each other into existence as has happened in some countries. Instead isolated individuals have been born on, or gone out and found, secret idylls where they have created their own ideals of accommodation. The 120 places found in this guide are all fantastic, but they took some finding. You could easily become blasé about this. Step off the Greenwood path and, although things are changing fast, you may find some fairly old-fashioned approaches to tourism lingering on.

But no need to dwell on that. You have the book in hand and therefore the wherewithal to enjoy Australia to the absolute full. Inside these pages lie the most humorous, friendly, warm Australians you could hope to meet. Here you will find great luxury, wonderful cooking, cutting-edge design… or if a place is not luxurious, then it will always be characterful, fun and owned by warm, unpretentious and humorous hosts. At its most fundamental we have been looking for places with 'soul', where you the guest are not just another bed night, but instead someone to be looked after, even befriended if that is what you want. The cardinal sin for us is a dearth of human care and attention.

EXPENSIVE DOES NOT MEAN GOOD

There are essentially two types of place to stay. There are those that fulfil their obligations in a commercial way and leave you feeling throughout your stay like the paying customer that you are. And there are those few great places where you are welcomed in and treated as a friend, cliché though this may now have become, and where paying at the end of your visit is a pleasurable surprise. (Oh, and of course there is a third category where paying for your stay is a disagreeable inevitability!)

It is a particular irony of the accommodation world that no price is ever put on the essential qualities of a place – people, atmosphere, charm. These terms are too woolly, perhaps, to quantify, but this is where one's real enjoyment of a place to stay stems from. You are asked to pay instead for tangible facilities like marble bathrooms and en-suite showers.

This is a fallacy that we try to dismantle in all our guides, which is why you will find places at all reasonable price levels. Expensive does not mean good. And nor does cheap (however appealing the word may sound!). If a place costs plenty then it will probably offer facilities in keeping with the price. But that does not mean you will have any fun. Some very expensive places forget that they are providing a service and look down their noses at their own guests. At the other end of the spectrum, the very cheapest places are often cheap for good reasons. Sometimes for spectacular reasons!

Character and genuine hospitality, the extra qualities we search for, are found spaced evenly across the price spectrum. Nowhere in this guide cuts corners at the risk of your displeasure. We give equal billing to each place we choose, no matter if it is a gorgeous lodge or a home-spun B&B.

At the top end, the most jewel-encrusted, nay 'boutique' places may drip with luxurious trimmings, but have retained their sense of atmosphere and humour, are friendly and informal and nearly all are still owned and managed by the same people. ('Boutique' always used to mean a 'small clothes shop in France', but it has sneaked into accommodation vocab somewhere along the line.)

Equally, there are places in the book that do not have much in the way of luxury, but easily compensate with unique settings, wonderful views and charming hosts.

It is the quality of experience that draws us in and this is not determined by how much you pay. In the end I know that you will really like the owners in this book, many of whom we now count as friends. And you will certainly make friends yourselves if you stick to the Greenwood trail.

Although this introduction is aimed mainly at self-propelling overseas travellers, Australians will love these places to stay just as much.

DRIVING
Not much to say about driving except that you may need to do quite a bit of it. Also if you are in Sydney and returning the car back to Sydney try Bayswater Cars on 02-9360-3622. I have always found them good value and efficient. Roads are in very good repair, as you would expect.

Kangaroos represent an obstacle to drivers, particularly at dusk when they are harder to see. They get dazzled by the headlights and can leap out like a rabbit in front of the car… except, of course, they are not rabbits, but kangaroos. So keep an eye out.

DIRECTIONS
We have provided directions, unless a 30-word spiel was unlikely to clarify matters, i.e. if a place is in the middle of a town or city. Most owners can fax detailed maps/directions or they will have a web site that can help.

PRICES AND PAYMENT
Prices are quoted in Australian dollars per couple sharing per night, unless specifically stated otherwise. Single rates are also given. We have provided a range to allow for expected price increases over two years. There might be unexpected increases if the property changes radically or exchange rates alter, in which case we would ask you to be understanding.

Quite a few places do not accept payment with credit cards – these have a 'CASH' symbol in the book – but may take travellers' cheques or other forms of payment. Again, ask when booking.

I K°∄∖∣ ∣
At the time of writing, the exchange rate was £1 = AUD$2.39.

MAPS
The maps in this book are not road maps, but merely indicators of where the properties are. You should get a detailed road map when you arrive.

CANCELLATION
Cancellation policies vary as much as the wallpaper and should be clarified on booking. Many establishments will ask for a credit card number when you book so that they are not wholly compromised if you fail to turn up.

SMOKING
It is most unlikely that anyone will want you to smoke indoors.

TELEPHONES
Calling Australia from abroad: the international dialling code is 61. So to call Australia from Britain, you key 00 61, then drop the 0 followed by the nine-digit phone number.

PAY FOR ENTRY
We could not afford to research and publish this guide in the way we do without the financial support of those we feature. Each place that we have chosen has paid an entry fee for which we make no apology. It has not influenced our decision-making about who is right or wrong for the guide and we turn down many more than we accept. The proof of this is in the proverbial pudding. Use the book and see for yourself. It is also very hard for us to write up a place that we are not enthusiastic about.

DISCLAIMER
We make no claims to god-like objectivity in assessing what is or is not special about the places we feature. They are there because we like them. Our opinions and tastes are mortal and ours alone. We have done our utmost to get the facts right, but apologise for any mistakes that may have slipped through the net. Some things change which are outside our control: people sell up, prices increase, exchange rates fluctuate, unfortunate extensions are added, marriages break up and even acts of God can rain down destruction. We would be grateful to be told about any errors or changes, however great or small. We can always make these editions on the web version of this book.

PLEASE WRITE TO US
Our email address is editor@greenwoodguides.com for all comments. We are always grateful to hear how much/little you enjoyed the places in the book.

We also have guides to New Zealand (new edition due at the end of 2003), Canada (in first edition) and South Africa (now in second edition, third edition due in May 2004). These books are available in bookshops or by emailing us direct.

Our web site address is www.greenwoodguides.com.

Indian

Ocean

Darwin

Legend for map pages
- ══ motorway & main roads
- ── secondary roads
- ── railway
- ═══ state boundary
- ----- national park
- ········ reserve
- ⊕ international airport
- ✈ regional airport

© Collins Bartholomew Ltd 2003

Broome

Nort

Tanami Desert

Terri

Great Sandy Desert

Alice Spring

Gibson Desert

W e s t e r n

A u s t r a l i a

Great Victoria Desert

9

Perth
Rockingham
Mandurah

S o u t h e r n   O c e a n

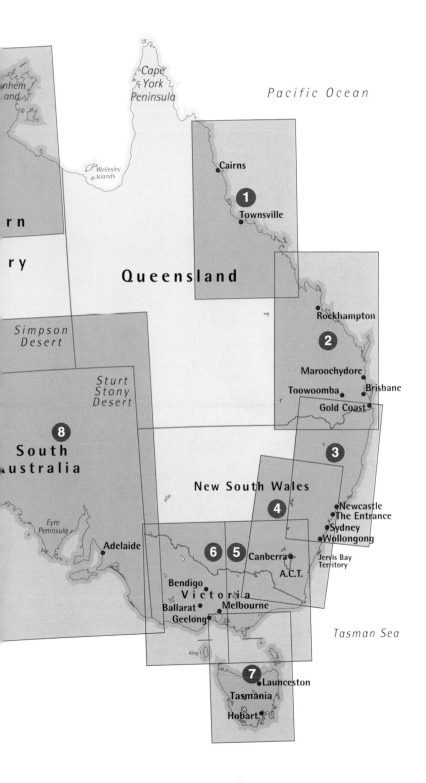

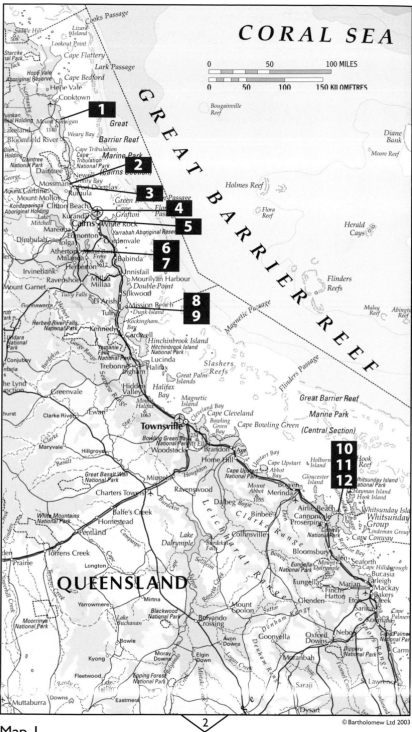

Map 1

© Bartholomew Ltd 2003

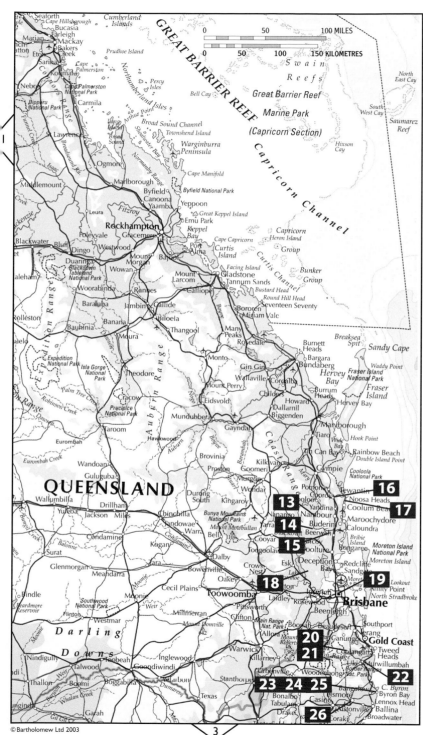

Map 2

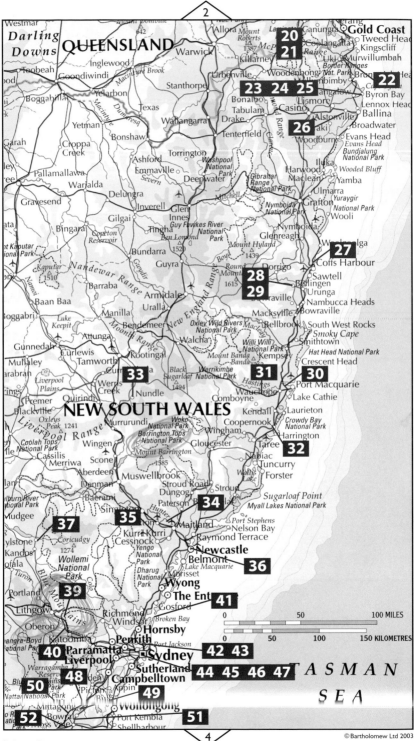

Map 3

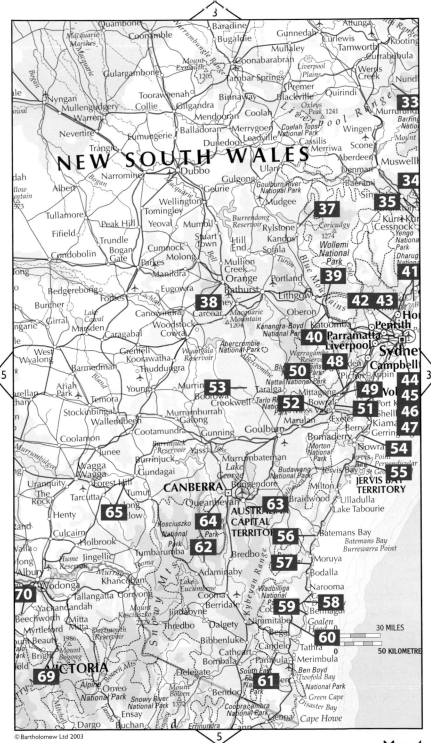

Map 4

© Bartholomew Ltd 2003

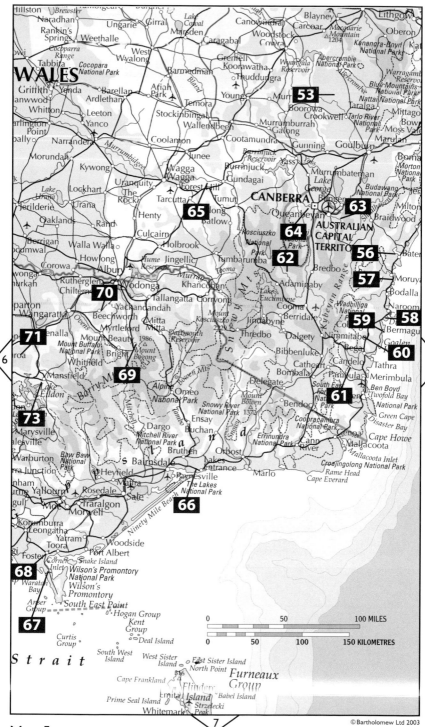

Map 5

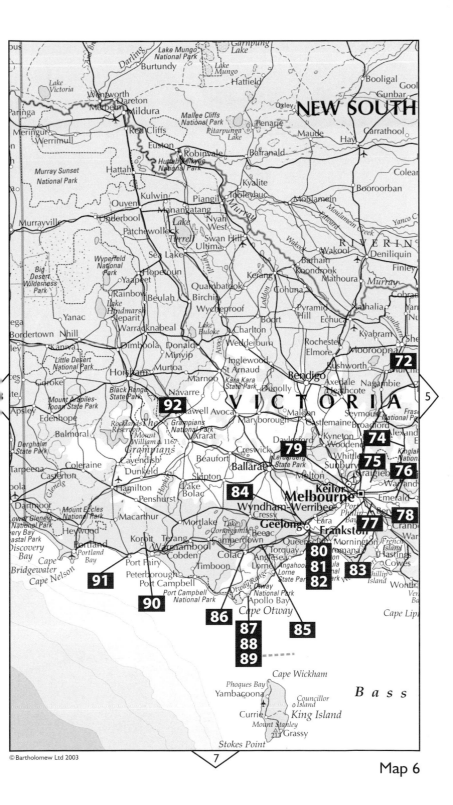

© Bartholomew Ltd 2003

Map 6

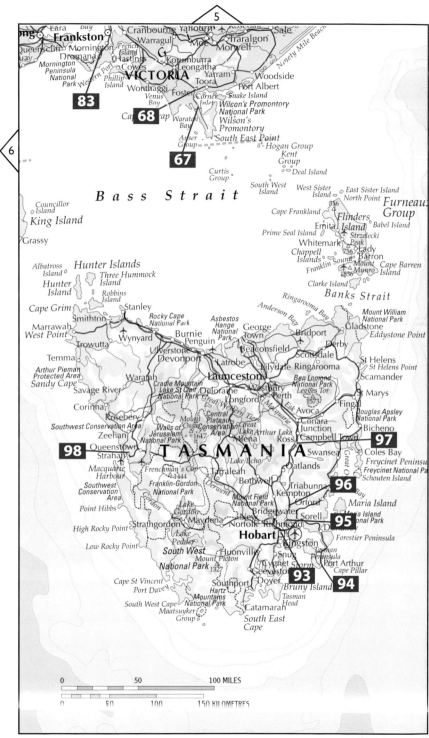

Map 7

© Bartholomew Ltd 2003

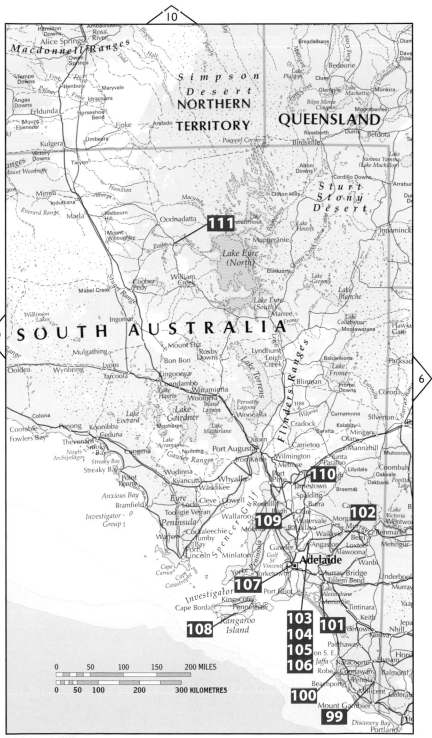

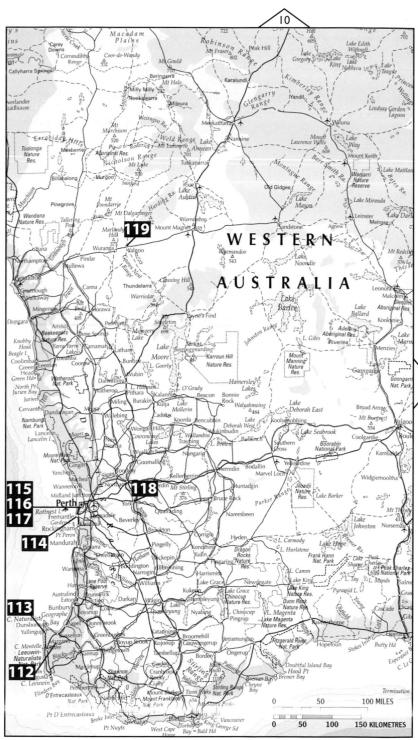

WESTERN

AUSTRALIA

119

115
116
117

114

113

112

118

Perth

| 0 | | 50 | | 100 MILES |

| 0 | 50 | 100 | 150 KILOMETRES |

Map 9

© Bartholomew Ltd 2003

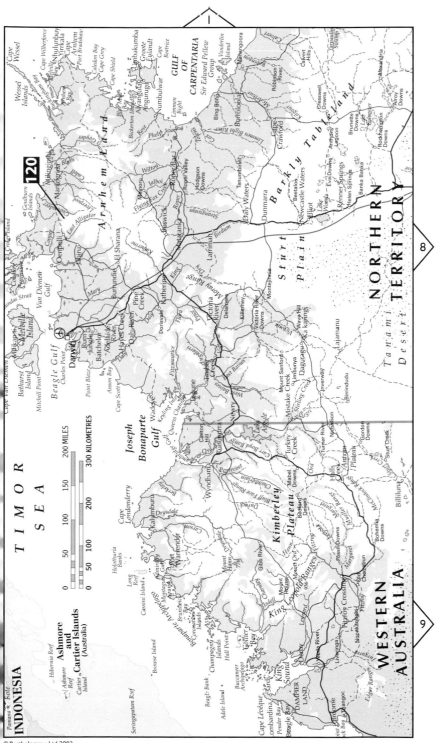

INDONESIA

Pamana • Fote

TIMOR SEA

Ashmore and Cartier Islands (Australia)

Hibernia Reef

Ashmore Reef
Cartier Island

Seringapatam Reef

Holothuria Banks

Long Reef

Cassini Island

Browse Island

Beagle Bank

Adele Island

0   50   100   150   200 MILES
0   50   100   200   300 KILOMETRES

Cape Van Diemen
Melville Island
Bathurst Island

Beagle Gulf
Darwin
Charles Point
Point Blaze

Van Diemen Gulf

Anson Bay
Cape Scott

Joseph Bonaparte Gulf

Queens Channel
Kalumburu
Cape Londonderry

Drysdale

Montague Sound
Prince Frederick
Harbour
Bigge Island
Coronation
Islands
Champagny Island
Hall Point

Buccaneer Archipelago

Cape Lévêque
Lombardina • Djarindjin
Pender Bay
Beagle Bay
King Sound

DAMPIER LAND

Derby

Fitzroy River

Elgar Range

GULF OF CARPENTARIA

Cape Wilberforce
Cape Wessel
Cape Wessel
Wessel Islands

Nhulunbuy • Yirrkala
Cape Arnhem
Port Bradshaw

Caledon Bay
Cape Grey
Cape Shield

Milingimbi
Goulburn Islands
Crocodile Island

Arnhem Land

Oenpelli
El Sharana
Jabiru
Batchelor
Adelaide River

Pine Creek
Katherine

Gunbalanya
Angururgu
Umbakumba
Groote Eylandt
Cape Boroloola

Bickerton Island
Bing Bong
Numbulwar
Limmen Bight

Sir Edward Pellew Group

NORTHERN TERRITORY

Sturt Plain

Barkly Tableland

Cresswell Downs
Brunette Downs
Rockhampton Downs
Anthony Lagoon

Newcastle Waters
Renner Springs
Helen Springs

Tanami Desert

Lajamanu

Balgo Hills

Banka Banka

WESTERN AUSTRALIA

Kimberley Plateau

Wyndham
Kununurra
Lake Argyle

Turkey Creek
Halls Creek

King Leopold Ranges

Fitzroy Crossing

© Bartholomew Ltd 2003

Map 10

Queensland

Peppers
Bloomfield Lodge

Managers: Peter and Pat MacPherson

Weary Bay, via Ayton 4871
Tel: 07-4035-9166
Fax: 07-4035-9180
Email:
pblres@peppers.com.au
Web: www.peppers.com.au

Queensland

The journey to Bloomfield is an adventure in itself, flying up the majestic North Queensland coast, then coming in low over the roof of the rainforest to land on a small grass airstrip. You swap plane for jeep and follow dirt roads to the river, finally boarding a launch that ferries you over Weary Bay to Bloomfield. It's an exciting, even hardy, trip, but at the end of it all you find the very lap of luxury, hidden away on the side of a hill where rainforest meets beach. The lodge is the hub – a big, open-plan room where you eat, drink, write postcards, read books. It is open to the breeze, with a palm-flanked swimming pool five paces ahead, an honesty bar six to the left and views through trees to the sea. Bedrooms are sprinkled around the hillside in timber cabins. They range in price, depending on size and view (some have sea views, others don't), but all have private balconies, timber floors and ceiling fans. All meals are included and I will go as far as to say that the food here was the best I had in Queensland. Various tours are included in the price (as is a return flight to Cairns). The rainforest walk is unmissable. Staff are remarkably friendly, informative and attentive. A great place to hide out.

Rooms: 17: 14 queens, 3 queens/twins; 4 queens have en-suite spa/shower, the others all have en-suite shower.
Price: Minimum 4-night stay recommended: from $1239 p.p. for 4 days, twin share. Includes all transfers from Cairns (including scenic flight).
Meals: All meals included in price. Drinks (and some optional trips) extra.
Directions: Flights leave from Hinterland Aviation in the General Aviation area of Cairns airport, usually at 9 a.m. Courtesy pick-up from your hotel is arranged.
Postal Address: PO Box 966, Cairns 4870.

Map Number: 1

Mossman Gorge B&B

Amanda Coxon
15 Gorge View Crescent, Mossman 4783
Tel: 07-4098-2497
Email: mossgorgebnb@austarnet.com.au
Web: www.bnbnq.com.au/mossgorge

Chris and Amanda have put hammocks on the wide decks, a sort of pre-emptive strike so th foot-weary guests can sit while they gaze. And the gazing, over the Drumsara sugar car plantation to the thickly-forested mountains of the lower Daintree National Park beyond, fabulous! The single-story, split-level home is at treetop level and, since it is built right on the ed of a steep rainforest hillside, very open, light and airy. There are binoculars for you to sp celebrities – the valley below is a popular film location – but mostly you will train them on th jungle flora and fauna. Some animals even frolic on the verandah. Amanda filled me in on th wildlife while I filled myself with warm, fluffy scones, cream and rosella fruit jam. The worlc biggest Hercules moths come here to feed on the bleeding heart trees (there is one next to th pool) and all year round huge, cobalt Ulysses and Cairns birdwing butterflies live here. Gia (harmless) 5-foot goannas, tiny blossom bats, honey-eaters (related to the hummingbirc kingfishers, rare rifle birds, grey goshawks and striped possums are all seen too. Chris rowed f Cambridge, is a dive master (he knows all the best spots on the reef) and in his spare time mac much of the furniture. Bedrooms are very comfortable and pretty with crisp linen. If you want learn more about Queensland, this is the place.

Rooms: 3: 1 queen with en/s shower, 2 doubles with en/s bath and shower.
Price: $85 – $120.
Meals: Very big Continental breakfast included. Dinner by arrangement. $20 for 1 course, $25 for 2 $30 for 3.
Directions: North into Mossman, then left at big sign for national park. Straight 1 km, then left into Coral Sea Drive. 1st right (Gorge View Crescent) an house ahead.
Postal Address: PO Box 1079, Mossman 4873.

Map Number:

House of Willow

Geoff and Julie Parmenter

42 Garrick Street, Port Douglas 4871
Tel: 07-4099-6265 Fax: 07-4099-6265
Email: info@houseofwillow.com.au Web: www.houseofwillow.com.au
Cell: 0418-692-194

Port Douglas is traditionally where the famous come to be ignored. It's the top Barrier Reef launch point, cosmopolitan and swanky, but typically Australian and down-to-earth too. For the low-down on golf courses and game fishing join Geoff as he feeds the tame grouper (which are fish, if you didn't know) down at his popular On the Inlet Seafood Restaurant at 5 p.m. each day. Julie, meanwhile, seems unimpressed by her own considerable interior design flair and organisational skills. All three houses under the Willow banner are as exquisite as they are unique. Private and open-plan, they are decorated in smooth Mediterranean colours with polished sandstone floors, bright rugs, woven willow couches piled with Versace cushions and dark violet bolsters. There are antiques, in-house water pools, giant metal sea-animal sculptures, massive and colourful photographs on the walls, marble-topped kitchens. The louver walls in the dining pavilions fold flat back so you can sit at the table and dip your toes in the pool. Jade lawns surround, verandahs drip bougainvillea. Basically, House of Willow is putting on the Ritz and is well prepared for the next Vogue shoot when it happens. *Watch the tiny honey-eaters make their hanging nest at the back door, walk right to the beach and left to cosmopolitan Port Douglas, both 1 minute away.*

Rooms: 3 houses. All with 3 x king rooms with en/s spa bathrooms; 1 king room has en/s shower only.
Price: $575 per house per night. Min 4-night stay in high season, negotiable at other times.
Meals: Chef or hampers can be arranged. Restaurants will deliver or are a 1-minute walk.
Directions: Emailed on booking.

Map Number: 1

3

Trinity on the Esplanade

Elise Warren
21 Vasey Esplanade, Trinity Beach, Cairns 4879
Tel: 07-4057-6850 Fax: 07-4057-8099
Email: stay@trinityesplanade.com Web: www.trinityesplanade.com

Elise's contemporary take on a traditional Queenslander brings to life a temple of cool elegance. This is a house that's big on space, small on clutter, with stylish and restful rooms throughout. Wander at will and you come across stone cherubs on plinths in bedrooms, ancient Indian pillars in the hall, flaming stainless-steel torches around the pool and a Balinese timber sofa in the gazebo. Bedrooms take your breath away. You sleep on the best linen, amid neutral earth colours on beds piled high with cushions. Doors lead out to small private courtyards, where you may find a plumped-up sofa or an ornate stone wall carving. The bridal suite has a four-poster in colonial style, wrapped up in a mosquito net. Bathrooms, likewise, are as good as they come, with the finest tiles, double showers and spa baths. And for those with an amour for glamour, the recently finished penthouse fills the upstairs level. It has a baby grand piano, an ancient Indian seat placed for the view, the swankiest of kitchens and an office in the tower. Breakfast on banana pancakes or poached eggs, with one eye on the sea scanning for dolphins. The beach starts across the road and if you turn left out of the front door, a two-minute stroll will take you past five good restaurants. Elise set up Cairns's night markets, so if you want to shop you know whom to ask.

Rooms: 7: 6 kings, all with en/s bath and shower. I penthouse suite has king with en/s spa and shower, and twins with en/s shower.
Price: $175 – $270. Penthouse $480 for 2 people, $600 for 4.
Meals: Full breakfast included.
Directions: North through Cairns, past airport, over next 7 roundabouts, left at 8th, signed Trinity Beach. Straight down to beach, then right and on right after 500 metres.

Map Number:

Birdwing B&B

Fern Pittman

13-15 Heavey Crescent, Whitfield, Cairns 4870
Tel: 07-4053-1615 Fax: 07-4053-1615
Email: info@birdwingretreat.com Web: www.birdwingretreat.com

I phoned Fern after a last-minute recommendation and, despite my faltering Greenwood Guide introduction, fifteen seconds later she still invited me to come and stay. Some people! Birdwing offers genuine, country-style hospitality in a beautiful environment. Fern runs a house and garden 'make-over' business and she designed and built the B&B cottage just over a year ago. It's all typical, modern Queensland practicality. The climate is so temperate that there's little need for walls; literally! The kitchen has only two, painted a deep lavender blue. On one there are all the cooking facilities you would want, on the other a low slung cane couch. Tall, wide leafed heliconias – both 'Sexy Pink' and 'Sexy Red' – and native gingers with fist-sized, solid cerise flowers droop right into the living area. The fridge is stocked with mouth-watering temptations that Fern purchases from the locals or you can breakfast on Fern-created pancakes and a healthy tropical breakfast that attests to the region's vast array of fruits. Bedrooms are butterfly-themed with hand-painted cushions on wide beds, contrasting linens, tiled floors and split-system air-conditioning. The garden is sculpted from the rainforest and the pool has no lights – great for skinny-dippers – and is surrounded by jasmine and mock orange, which release a heavy scent at night. All this and only a short roo bounce from the city. *9 mins to the airport or Cairns.*

Rooms: 2: 1 king plus sofa-bed and 1 king/twin, both with en/s bath and shower.
Price: From $115 – $125. Extra person $10 per night. Stay for 6 nights and the 7th is free.
Meals: Continental breakfast included.
Directions: From the airport drive to the Cook Hwy, turn left. Then immediately turn right into Collins Avenue. At the end of Collins turn right at the roundabout into Woodward St. Turn right into Jensen St at the Bowling Club then first left into Heavey Crescent.

Mt Quincan Crater Retreat

Barb and Kerry Kehoe
Peeramon Rd, Yungaburra, Atherton 4872
Tel: 07-4095-2255 Fax: 07-4095-2255
Email: kehoe@mtquincan.com.au Web: www.mtquincan.com.au

What!? On the rim of a volcano? Our brave inspector almost faltered. Barb and Kerry have bu
six amazing, self-contained stilt houses on the very edge of the steep rim. Four face th
surrounding farmland and other distant (and less exclusive) volcanoes. Two face into the crate
but, *calmez-vous*, the volcano is dormant and its centre is a water marsh, home to much nativ
wildlife living in their own private eco-system just under your nose. Endangered tree-climbin
kangaroos make their home here, as do bandicoots, but you don't have to look down for them
just out, since you really are in the tree canopy. Each house is very private. There is one majo
wall at the back, but the rest is designed to make the view as seamless as possible. There is lo
of glass between upright polished stakes that support high vaulted ceilings. There are swivellin
wood-burners, double spa baths, deep beds, red kitchens full of fresh roses, bowls of local fru
and three cabins have funky outside showers. Breakfast is a hamper full of good country fare: loc
fruits, honey, breads and even proper pork sausages. You are spoiled by the loveliest of hosts an
after you've been given your welcome basket – home-baked muffins, booties in winter, choc
and port – they will fill you in on what to do in the Tablelands area. *Laundry facilities in each cabir*

Rooms: 6: all have king beds with en/s shower; 3
have outdoor showers.
Price: $195 – $275 (minimum 2-night stay).
Meals: Full breakfast provisions are included for you
to cook yourself. Dinners by arrangement: $30 p.p.
(excluding wine) for a 3-course hamper.
Directions: From Yungaburra drive past the Shell
Garage (on your right). After about 1.5km turn right
down Peeramon Rd. Follow it for 2.5km. Turn right
into Hunt Rd and Mt Quincan is on the left.
Postal Address: PO Box 200, Yungaburra 4872.

Map Number:

Allumbah Pocket Cottages

Keith and Janet Mole

24-26 Gillies Highway, Yungaburra 4884
Tel: 07-4095-3023 Fax: 07-4095-3300
Email: info@allumbahpocketcottages.com.au
Web: www.allumbahpocketcottages.com.au

I came to Yungaburra blind to the treats that litter the area, but Keith soon put me straight. The Atherton Tablelands are apparently the same size as Tasmania (!) and Yungaburra sits central to it all, capital perhaps of Queensland's waterfalls, volcanoes and high plateaux. "We wanted to keep everything uncluttered and comfortable," says Janet of their cottages. And that's what they've done. The white weatherboard cabins have a simple, smart, country look: pale cream and blue walls and crisp cotton linens, polished floors, a kitchen(ette) area, potbelly wood-burner stoves, thick merino wool blankets and bathroom with spas. I plonked down and absorbed the last of the golden sunset from the deck; a great place, too, to devour your breakfast of home-made cob bread, preserves and jams, organic milk and eggs that are left each morning in a wicker hamper. Deep gravel paths are bordered first by long lines of irises, then by box hedging and mock orange blossoms, planted for their hazy evening scent, while lawns encircle the heated jacuzzi pagoda. Janet and Keith also run an information centre so can answer all your questions on exactly what to do first, like viewing platypuses just a minute's walk away. It's all just an hour from Cairns and, as the region's brochure says, "2500 feet above your worries!" *They also have two bigger, separate houses in the village. Peterson Creek two minutes, good restaurants all but next door.*

Rooms: 8 self-contained cottages: 6 with one bedroom (king bed) and en/s shower and spa bath, 2 with 2 bedrooms (1 with queen and 2 singles, 1 with 2 x queen) and shower.
Price: 1-bed apartments (sleep 2): $190. 2-bed cottages (sleep up to 4): $225. Reduced rates for longer stays.
Meals: Continental breakfast is included. Restaurants are a 1-minute walk.
Directions: Well sign-posted and smack in the middle of Yungaburra village. Number 24-26 on the main highway from Atherton to Gordonvale.
Postal Address: PO Box 213, Yungaburra 4884.

Map Number: 1

Villa Zara

Vicki and Steve Wiltshire
77 Holt Rd, Brooks Beach 4852
Tel: 07-4088-6699 Fax: 07-4088-6020
Email: accom@missionbeachholidays.com.au
Web: www.missionbeachholidays.com.au Cell: 0419-021-134

Villa Zara is wonderfully unusual, something of a stone-age temple sitting up on the bedrock and looking down over its own (almost) private beach. Crafted by a local builder-cum-sculptor, the structure is made almost wholly from sculpted concrete. The walls are all free-form, with large windows which create the impression that the tropical garden is growing into the rooms; elsewhere, walls simply do not exist, in order to make the most of the view. The main lodge/kitchen area has glamorous beach aspects with giant cushions, wide window-seats, fireplace and timber poles supporting a vaulted roof and glass doors which slide back to views straight ahead to the reef. Step right to the deep sunken pool. Head left along pink paths down to two separate sleeping/living areas. My favourite was the shack closest to the surf. With a curious indoor/outdoor shower that you share with tropical irises, bright yellow and blue beds draped in mosquito nets and a rope-and-trap-door option to your own upstairs lounge, it's hard to do the place justice. *14km of sandy beach at the end of the garden, cassowaries in it. Dunk Island ferry terminal 5 mins drive. Mission Beach Village 9.5km. Children over 12 years welcome.*

Rooms: 3: all queens with en-suite showers. Single-party bookings only.
Price: From $250 – $350 per couple. Min 2-night stay. Stays of more then 3 nights decrease the amount by $50 per night.
Meals: Self-catering, although catering services can be arranged.
Directions: Emailed on booking.
Postal Address: PO Box 54, Mission Beach 4853.

Map Number:

Sejala on the Beach

Queensland

Janet Norgate
1 Pacific Parade, Mission Beach 4852
Tel: 07-4088-6699 Fax: 07-4088-6020
Email: sales@sejala.com.au or tikwis@bigpond.net.au
Web: www.sejala.com.au

Not much has changed at Sejala since the first edition, except that Vicki is now managing the property. She is great fun and as an estate agent in the area knows it all inside out and back to front... even the islands. Mission Beach is still a relatively sleepy place, but it's being discovered slowly. Hardly surprising since this village paradise squeezes itself between thick rainforest on one side and miles of white sand and the ocean on the other. If the British TV show "I'm a Celebrity – Get me Out of Here" means anything to you... well, the girls came to Sejala to relax! The pink and purple beach shacks epitomise beach-funky. Two are thirty metres from the beach; the other takes refuge by the pool. All are cool and tropical with distressed wood floors, sofas facing seawards, bamboo matting and Mediterranean colours, barbecues and painted decks. The bathrooms are tremendous with showers in sculpted, corrugated-iron booths and walls that open up to the garden. It is self-catering here, although Vicki (who can organize anything from car hire to reef trips) can sort out hampers of treats for you. But 500 metres away you'll find Mission Beach village and its many restaurants. A great place to wash up... I mean Sejala, not the restaurants. *Children 12+ welcome. Great Barrier Reef, wreck-diving, tropical islands, white-water rafting, kayaking, horse-riding in the rainforest with the cassowaries, sky-diving and crocodile spotting.*

Rooms: 3 beach huts, each with queen beds and en/s showers.
Price: $165 – $200.
Meals: Hampers for breakfast or dinners can be arranged.
Directions: From Townsville leave the Bruce Hwy just north of Tully for Mission Beach. From Cairns leave Bruce Hwy at El Arish. At Mission Beach take Seaview St towards beach, 2nd right into Pacific Pde, then 1st left and signed right.

Whitsunday Moorings B&B

Peter Brooks
37 Airlie Crescent, Airlie Beach 4802
Tel: 07-4946-4692 Fax: 07-4946-4692
Email: info@whitsundaymooringsbb.com.au
Web: www.whitsundaymooringsbb.com.au

Peter, an English Sydneysider, moved up to Airlie Beach three years ago (a retirement present) and now spends his days instructing gardeners, watching the cricket, boating and strolling around Airlie – an Englishman abroad. He lives at the top of the hill, less than half a kilometre from the beach, with outstanding views across the water and islands. In the morning you can count the boats out as you sit on the shaded verandah and have breakfast. At night, take your glass of wine and count them back in. Breakfast is a feast – you should allow a leisurely hour for it. Wedgewood china stands on crisp linen and you get tropical fruit, fresh juices, cereals and mueslis, bacon and eggs, toast and the company of a flock of rainbow lorikeets. Bedrooms are suites, with terracotta tiles, bamboo, ceiling fans (and air-con), cedar wood blinds, rugs, big beds (with starched sheets) sofas and screens so you can sleep with the doors open. Both rooms open onto their own verandah and there is also a pool shaded by a pompoo tree and flanked by flowers that shed their petals in the water. Peter will happily advise and book trips: you can dive or snorkel on the Great Barrier Reef, sail among the 74 Whitsunday islands, fish, whale-watch or head to Cedar Falls and swim in fall-fed rock pools.

Rooms: 2 doubles, both with en/s shower.
Price: From $130. Singles from $115.
Meals: Full breakfast included. Other meals available locally.
Directions: Into Airlie, past sign for Able Point Marina, over crest, 1st right, 1st right again (Airlie Crescent) and on right at crest of hill.
Postal Address: PO Box 394, Airlie Beach 4802.

Map Number: 1

Whitsunday Private Yacht Charters

Ian and Maree Lawson

Office 18, Abel Point Marina, Airlie Beach 4802
Tel: 07-4946-6880 Fax: 07-4946-4943
Email: wpyc@whitsunday-yacht.com.au
Web: www.whitsunday-yacht.com.au

You might not have considered hiring a boat when you go up to Queensland, but I recommend this adventurous option to even the most inexperienced sailors. The charter company will hold your hand and even provide crew if needed (at an additional cost). After a morning's briefing you will be given the helm and off you sail, around 74 exquisite islands fringed with coral reef and white-sand beaches. The Whitsundays straddle the Great Barrier Reef and you will spend your days snorkelling and diving on the reefs, swimming with dolphins off the boat… or lounging on deck eating Bounty bars. There are 8 island resorts, all with gorgeous swimming pools, some with golf courses, offering overnight moorings (priced per boat: about $66 for Hamilton Island, $45 for Daydream) or you can drop anchor in one of the many bays and coves. All craft are equipped with snorkelling gear, linen, radios (you log in twice daily), hot water, fridge, CD players, BBQ and even motorised dinghies. Vessels can be fully catered or you BYO food (some islands have restaurants too). State-of-the-art boats range from cruising or performance sailing yachts with wooden interiors, to sailing catamarans with huge deck space and motor cruisers for non-sailors. The boats are excellent value for a group and 5 nights (minimum hire) are just enough to see the area. *Fuel for cruisers about $30 – $40 a day depending on boat size. Kids welcome.*

Rooms: 18 sailing yachts and catamarans, 31 – 43 ft (2 – 10 people) and 2 motor cruisers (2 – 8 people), all with private cabins and showers; larger boats have 2 bathrooms.
Price: Per vessel per night: $360 – $1000 depending on vessel size; ie. approx $100 – $130 p.p. per night for groups of 4+ pax, a little more for just 2. Fuel/resort island charges extra.
Meals: Gourmet packages available or BYO – full kitchen facilities on board.
Directions: Into Airlie from Proserpine. Marina signed left when you first see the sea. Go into Marina village.
Postal Address: PO Box 800, Airlie Beach 4802.

Map Number: 1

Solway Lass

Allen Grundy

Shop 1, 4 The Esplanade,
Airlie Beach 4802
Tel: 07-4946-6577
Fax: 07-4946-6133
Email: info@solwaylass.com
Web: www.solwaylass.com

Solway Lass is a magnificent, century-old, yo-ho-ho-style Tall Ship powered by 5500 square feet of white sails. What more exciting way to explore the 74-island dreamland of the Whitsundays. The captain makes a perfect Hornblower and the crew interchange so service is always tip-top. You can choose to get involved and help haul the yard or sit back and be entertained by the pirate antics, hear the amazing history of 'The Lass', snorkel and dive the coral reefs and laze in the bow net. Routes vary depending on the weather and the captain's whim. You will swim the best snorkelling spots, visit windless and unspoilt white-sand beaches, spot sea eagles, find dolphins or turtles and – in season – watch humpback whales. The boat can take up to 70 on board, but the cabin refit has been tailored for 32 guests in 11 oak-and-cedar-lined cabins. There are good-sized double and single beds, brass lamps to light your way and bathrooms are spic and span. Meals are freshly prepared and plentiful: a Continental breakfast, cold-meat buffet or BBQ with salads and pastas for lunch, while dinners are hot and vary with the season. There's a rope swing for those that are feeling courageous, a cat-o-nine-tails for those found misbehaving and a fully licensed bar. *Special diets catered for.*

Rooms: 127ft Tall Ship with 11 cabins for 32 guests. 1 x 6 share, 3 x 4 share, 5 x double/twin, 1 x double 1 x twin. Bathrooms are shared, with separate men's/women's facilities.
Price: Min 3-day trip, max 6 days. 3-night trip in dbl cabin is $429 – $459 p.p. Includes all meals, snorkelling equipment, local courtesy transfers. Park fees extra.
Meals: Breakfast, lunch, dinner and snacks all incl'd. .... Into Airlie from Proserpine. Through main street and left into The Esplanade. Shop 1 is on the right.
Postal Address: PO Box 981, Airlie Beach, Whitsunday 4802.

Map Number:

Spotted Chook Ferme Auberge

Jane and Leeroy Hutton
176 Western Avenue, Montville 4560
Tel: 07-5442-9242 Fax: 07-5478-5811
Email: mail@spottedchook.com Web: www.spottedchook.com

Staying at the Spotted Chook is like visiting your best friend who happens to live in a five-star hotel. Inspired by their long travels in France and Austria, Leeroy and Jane created this sprawling, colourful inn themselves. Built on poles along the side of a hill and split-level throughout, bedroom windows and antique doors fling open to wide verandahs. From here you peek through the tree canopy to views over the valley and the Baroon Pocket Dam. The large beds are hand-made and individually dressed with bold-coloured linens; the bathtubs are claw-foot or sunken and the sofas proper and feathery. Chickens crop up all over the place, sometimes real, sometimes as topiary, paintings or sculptures. For dinner you will be offered a mouth-watering and inventive menu, which might include Gympie goat's cheese and asparagus wrapped in Parma ham and served with a macadamia nut dressing or Moreton Bay bugs (a shellfish) with herb fettuccine and chilli cream sauce. Breakfast is no less decadent with blueberry pancakes, eggs Benedict and fluffy omelettes on offer. The chooks (and Blackberry the sheep) have technically been banned from the house so there should be buckets of roses sitting on the old pine tables. There is nowhere quite like this. *Wake to mist in the valley, native birdsong in the rainforest, swimming at the bottom of the paddocks, fishing in the lake.*

Rooms: 4: 1 queen with double sofa-bed and en/s shower and bath; 1 qn with sgl sofa-bed and en/s sh and bath; 1 qn with en/s bath; 1 qn with 2 sgls, en/s sh and bath (family room).
Price: From $180 per night, min 2 nights. One-night stays from $250.
Meals: Breakfast is included. Dinners are available by arrangement, from $60 p.p. excluding wine.
Directions: 1 hour north of Brisbane. Take Bruce Hwy and exit at Glasshouse Mountains. Turn off at Landsborough then follow the Maleny road, taking the Montville turn. Just before the Montville shops turn L into Western Avenue. 1.8km to house on L.
Postal Address: PO Box 98 Montville 4560.

Lyola Pavilions in the Forest

Leisa Solomon and John Martinkovic
198 Policeman Spur Road,
Maleny 4552
Tel: 07-5429-6900
Email: stay@lyola.com.au
Web: www.lyola.com.au

Lyola is an eleven out of ten! You're at the end of the track, on the side of a hill, with views across lush rainforest to rising mountains in the distance. You are surrounded by trees in which koalas come to breed and if you follow the path into the rainforest, you will come to a natural swimming pool in a stream that comes with its own waterfall. All around you is forest – you hear only natural sounds... apart from the gasps of newly-arrived guests as they enter their pavilions. There are two of them, "Hide" and "Seek", and they are both magnificent. "Seek", its interior a pallet of energising colours, stands on poles ten metres high in the forest and faces an expansive view of the valley beyond. "Hide", in chic claret and forest hues, has a very private shower outside in the rainforest. It's a luxury overdose: candles in bathrooms, piles of cushions on sleigh beds, bamboo foot rests, the best cotton linen, pampering aromatherapy products, day beds to lounge on, bathrobes to lounge in. Best of all are the sliding walls of glass that open up completely, bringing the rainforest into the sitting-room. You can go to bed at night with the doors open, the screens drawn, and fall asleep to the sound of the valley. Lyola is also properly eco-accredited, a hard-to-get accolade that very few have the initiative and drive to achieve. *Mountain bikes available.*

Rooms: 2 pavilions, both with queen beds, en-suite spa bath and shower, fireplace and kitchen.
Price: $200 – $270. Minimum 2-night stay at weekends.
Meals: Breakfast provisions provided. Complimentary wine and regional cheese platter on arrival. Restaurants nearby.
Directions: From Landsborough towards Maleny up the range. Turn left onto Tourist Drive No 23 and left again towards Woodford for 5.5km, right onto Policeman Spur Rd then follow signs.
Postal Address: PO Box 418 Maleny 4552.

The Eyrie

Peter and June Rogers

316 Brandenburg Rd, Bald Knob 4552
Tel: 07-5494-8242 Fax: 07-5439-9666
Email: jollyrogers@eyrie-escape.com.au Web: www.eyrie-escape.com.au

The Eyrie is simply outstanding – on all counts. Ex-Somerset and ex-Sydneysider Peter seems to know everyone and within minutes we found (most do apparently) that we shared friends. He and June renovated the honey-coloured timber house making it one room deep, filling it with antiques and adding a sheet-glass window along the whole front wall to make the most of possibly the best view in the Glass House Mountains. Guest rooms are large and sophisticated and all open from the verandah on one side through to private terraces and the view on the other. The marble bathrooms are exemplary, as are the bedrooms generally. June is a fantastic chef and, behind a glass wall that trickles with water, bustled away in the kitchen, seamlessly producing a five-star banquet. I had to drag myself away from the final round of smooth cheeses, fruits, home-made truffles, tokay, liqueurs, laughter and stories and head to bed. The house really does perch peak top on a slice of land that drops away steeply on all sides (the pool, spa and tennis court do too and it could take some time to retrieve a wayward tennis ball). The distant ocean shimmers beyond the Sunshine Coast and the forested coastal plain stretches from the city fringes to the base of the Eyrie cliff. Lightning storms and sunrises are magnificent. *Peter offers a taxi service from nearby restaurants. Glass House Mountains and Australia Zoo 10 mins.*

Rooms: 3: 2 doubles, both with en/s shower; 1 twin/double, en/s bath and shower.
Price: $195 – $240. Singles less 25%.
Meals: Full breakfast incl'. Dinner 2 courses $40 p.p. (exc' wine), 3 courses $82.50 (inc' wine). Guests' friends not staying: $30 (2 c, exc' wine) – $60 (3c, inc' w).
Directions: From Landsborough to Maleny. After about 5km, right (after turn-off to Peachester) into Hovard Rd. Right into Brandenburg Rd. Continue for 2km and signed left.
Postal Address: PO Box 6117, Mooloolah 4553.

Cudgerie Homestead

Jenny and David Mathers
42 Cudgerie Drive, Cooroy 4563
Tel: 07-5442-6681 Fax: 07-5442-6681
Email: cudgerie@hotmail.com Web: www.cudgerie.com
Cell: 0408-982-461

This is a classic Greenwood find: informal, homely, brilliantly run and very charismatic. Your host
gave up the London finance markets and came home to host. And they excel. David is original
Tasmanian, then had a spell in Europe, then Africa… before finally he swapped baking in th
deserts for baking desserts (ow!). Yes, they are rather good at cooking too. No sooner had
frosted glass of Jenny's lemonade arrived than a selection of delicacies was placed before me
most memorable among which were a melt-in-the-mouth Middle Eastern orange cake an
squares of chocolate hazelnut panforte. You can even pick your own custard apples, lychee
bananas, mulberries and macadamia nuts in season. David's dishes are always locally sourced,
not home-grown, and a typical example of a main course at dinner might be chargrilled swordfis
steak on cauliflower purée with oven-roasted tomatoes. The 100-year-old house sits pretty
the top of a verdant valley and the grounds, landscaped to include a vogueish swimming po
surrounded by wide wooden decking, look over grassy pastures and fruit trees. Back inside, a
open-plan, funky kitchen separates the family's area from the guests'. Bedrooms are country-sty
with white downy duvets, cane and wicker chairs and gingham cushions and all but one ope
onto the enveloping verandah. *Noosa's beaches and Eumundi markets are nearby.*

Rooms: 3: 1 queen with en-suite shower; 1 double
and 1 twin with en/s shower; 1 queen with private
shower.
Price: $150 – $170. Single $80 – $95.
Meals: Full breakfast included. Dinners from $50 pe
person excluding wine. Picnic hampers $25 per
person. Lunch from $30 p.p.
Directions: Cudgerie Homestead is in the
Hinterland 20 minutes from Noosa. Turn off the
Bruce Highway onto Black Mountain Range Rd, the
left onto Cudgerie Drive after 1.5km. Homestead is
250m on the right.

Map Number:

Lake Weyba Cottages

Philip and Sam Brown

79 Clarendon Road, Peregian Beach, Sunshine Coast 4573
Tel: 07-5448-2285 Fax: 07-5448-2285
Email: info@lakeweybacottages.com
Web: www.lakeweybacottages.com

Queensland

Set on twenty beautiful acres on the shores of Lake Weyba, Philip and Sam's cottages provide a natural pick-me-up, blitzing fatigue and clearing cluttered minds. They spent several years running ski hotels in France before heading to Noosa to swap snow for sun and establish their new lives. The result? Six wooden chalets, all with timber floors and verandahs, facing a stunning, transparent, natural pool with a white sandy beach on one side. You will probably spend most of your time out here – this is Queensland after all – breakfasting on the deck, smiling politely at the birdlife, eyeing the kangaroos. Newspapers and a homemade breakfast are delivered each morning and I was cranked into life by muffins, scrambled eggs, smoked salmon, grilled tomatoes, fruit, yoghurt and fresh OJ. No wonder the birds looked so interested. During the day there are mountain bikes, fishing rods and canoes to be borrowed, beaches and lakes to be explored and markets to be inspected. The evening line-up is more luxurious; a double spa (each chalet has one), wood fire (air-con for summer) and an immaculate bed draped with mosquito nets combine to see you happily through to the next morning. *Beaches, Noosa and Eumundi markets within 10 minutes. Hosted trips on site include bird-watching, star-gazing and a canoe-and-picnic tour.*

Rooms: 6 self-contained cottages: 1 king/twin, 4 queen, 1 with king/twin and queen. All with en/s shower and separate spa. New honeymoon cottage from Dec 2003.
Price: $195 – $260.
Meals: Full breakfast included. Dinners from $45 p.p. (excluding wine) can be served to your cottage.
Directions: Head toward Noosa on the Sunshine Motorway, turn right into Murdering Creek Rd, then the 3rd turn-off to the left and it's on the left again.

Map Number: 2

Mount Glorious Getaway Cottages

Margaret and Sam Brown

Browns Rd, Mt Glorious 4520
Tel: 07-3289-0172 Fax: 07-3289-0072
Email: relax@mtgloriousgetaways.com.au
Web: www.mtgloriousgetaways.com.au

The Brown family has been here long enough to have the road named after them, although in fairness it is no great act of vanity as it leads nowhere but their land. Sam's father bought a weekender here in the 1940s, which opened up the land a little bit, but you are still pretty much at the top of a mountain, bang in the middle of the Maiala National Park, with rainforest all around. Red cedar, black bean and flooded gum trees all stand serene, home to rosellas, bower birds, golden whistlers, honey-eaters and rarer birds like the sooty owl and marbled frogmouth. Other often-seen forest critters are pademelons (small wallabies), water and forest dragons (goannas), butterflies and green tree frogs. Sam and Margaret hail from the outback, but chose Mt Glorious to retire to. Sam built four mountainside chalets, positioning them for the best views through treetops to the distant sea. Inside, they are warm and woody: wood-burners, high ceilings, fresh garden flowers, comfy beds, pretty fabrics... rather like a ski lodge, just without the snow. Very much without the snow in fact. Outside you'll find old plough-disc barbecues and decks on which to sit and do very little indeed – listen to the birds, relax, read. Rainforest downpours are spectacular, forest mists roll in. The mountain closes down at night, so BYO food (each cottage has a kitchen) or Margaret can provide excellent deli meals and breakfasts.

Rooms: 4: 3 x 1-bed cottages and 1 x 3-bed cottage, all with en/s shower.
Price: Weekends: $160 per couple per night, min 2 night stay. Mid-week: $140 per couple per night. Reductions for longer stays.
Meals: Either self-cater or breakfast hampers and deli meals can be provided.
Directions: From Samford follow signs to Mt Glorious. Right at T-junction, through Mt Glorious village and signed right after 1km.

Map Number:

Annerley B&B "Ridge Haven"

Peter and Morna Cook
374 Annerley Rd, Annerley, Brisbane
Tel: 07-3391-7702 Fax: 07-3392-1786
Email: ridgehaven@uq.net.au Web: www.uqconnect.net/ridgehaven

Ridge Haven is a 140-year-old 'Queenslander', Aussie-speak for a traditional weatherboard home, ringed by verandahs and designed to catch whatever summer breezes are on offer. French doors open into all rooms and Peter and Morna have also built a wide back deck to entice you to take breakfast among the tropical parrots, potted herbs, overhanging palms and pink- and orange-flowering bougainvillaea. They live downstairs with Danny their dog. Ridge Haven is the very model of a traditional B&B: wholesome, friendly and good value. Morna used to run a catering company and now puts those skills to good use at breakfast, where delights might be bircher muesli, home-made stewed fruits, jams and home-made breads, stuffed field mushrooms and devilled kidneys… or whatever you want. Bedrooms are neat and comfortable with lace and block-out curtains to hide the Queensland sun, for those needing to rest up after a long flight. Beds have decorative mosquito nets, throws, cream carpets and tidy bathrooms with slate-walled showers. Elsewhere there are antiques, a TV alcove in the guest lounge and a pretty music stand – but you'll have to BYO instruments. *Restaurants nearby, airport 25 mins, city centre under 10 mins.*

Rooms: 3: 2 queens (1 has extra single bed) and 1 double. All with en/s shower.
Price: From $95 – $135.
Meals: Tropical or cooked gourmet breakfast included.
Directions: From Brisbane airport follow signs to city. In Fortitude Valley, take route to Story Bridge. This road becomes Mains Ave then Ipswich Rd. Turn R off Ipswich into Torrens St (at McDonald's). Then L into Annerley. Ridge Haven is in 4th block along.

The Mouse's House

Alexandra and Russell Quigley

2807 Springbrook Road, Springbrook 4213
Tel: 07-5533-5192 Fax: 07-5533-5411
Email: info@mouseshouse.com.au Web: www.mouseshouse.com.au

The Mouse's House is in the rainforest – not in a clearing in the rainforest, but *in* the rainforest. was lucky enough to get a storm on the night I stayed and afterwards, outside in the darkness, th forest started to sing or so it seemed to me. The creek slid by below, while possums and suga gliders chattered in the canopy. Enchanting stuff. When daylight comes, the forest is dense enoug to keep all but the smallest chink of light from its floor. Hidden away somewhere within are eleve chalets. When you arrive, you bundle all your luggage into trolleys and trundle along the path through the trees, perhaps stopping to allow a luminous blue crayfish to pass – they get right (way. When, eventually, you enter your hideaway you find a world of wood: floor, walls an ceiling, even the sofas and beds all come from the forest. There are beamed cathedral ceiling rugs on the floor and a wood-burner already smouldering. Each is warm and cosy and if yc rummage around, you'll find thick blankets, bathrobes, Monopoly, decks of cards and new DV players. Pull yourself away and walk – there are great tracks in the area, such as the Twin Fal circuit. Alternatively, follow jostling signposts in Springbrook and head for the look-outs. Bac home, there's also a sauna and a plunge pool in the middle of the rainforest.

Rooms: 11 chalets, 8 with spas and 3 with showers
Price: $150 – $175. Minimum 2 nights.
Meals: Full kitchen facilities to self-cater.
Directions: 30 minutes from Mudgeeraba, south west for Springbrook. When you reach town keep going straight through Springbrook for 4 km and house located on left.

Map Number: 2 &

Forget-Me-Not Cottages

Andrew and Lynette Moore

20 Pine Creek Rd, Springbrook 4213
Tel: 07-5533-5150 Fax: 07-5533-5175
Email: forget@onthenet.com.au Web: www.forgetmenot.com.au
Cell: 0417-623-123

Andrew had even managed to organise a rainbow for when I arrived. He and Lynette live with their three children high in the mountains on twenty lush hectares of farmland plateau an hour from Brisbane in a World-Heritage-listed National Rainforest Park. It's very private… if you ignore the koalas, wallabies, kangaroos, horses and dogs. And the parrots and lorikeets which swarm the ancient, purple-flowering jacaranda trees in the summer evenings. The views from the two cottages are so good that, when renovating, they made the front walls almost entirely of glass, so now you can drink your uninterrupted fill of the rainforest canopy and the rugged mountains. The cottages epitomise casual country chic with a practical edge and are immaculately styled and beautifully furnished, the smaller in pinks and greens, the other in blue and cream. They have wide, polished floors, double spas in the bathrooms and unpainted wooden dressers in the all-you-could-want kitchen. The cottage garden's deck is well placed for brunch-time sun (and Lynette will do a gourmet, mostly-home-made breakfast hamper) but the front deck was built for the sunsets. Whilst sampling the gourmet biscuits and truffles on offer, Andrew and I settled back into the deep stripy couches and chatted about golfing in the Loire and in-house aromatherapy massages. *Springbrook National Park 5 mins, 12 waterfalls all nearby.*

Rooms: 2 self-contained cottages, both with queen beds and en-suite spa and shower.
Price: From $200 – $240 per cottage per night.
Meals: Breakfast by arrangement. Provisions for Continental $16 p.p., full $20 p.p. Dinners by arrangement: from $50 p.p. (including wine).
Directions: From the Pacific Hwy take the Springbrook Rd. At Pine Creek Rd turn right and head up to the top of the hill. Forget-Me-Not is signposted on the left and is the second house from the top.

New South Wales

Wollumbin Palms Retreat

Roger and Margaret Ealand

112 Mt Warning Rd, Mt Warning, via Murwillumbah 2484
Tel: 02-6679-5063 Fax: 02-6679 5278
Email: wollpalm@norex.com.au Web: www.wollumbinpalms.com.au

There are three lodges at Wollumbin, each so extraordinary that you will want to try them all. In 'Altwood', a luxurious cave, you can lie in bed and gaze out through a wall of glass to the peak of Mount Warning, where the first ray of morning sun hits Australia. Alternatively, in 'Kings' you can sit on your covered verandah during the odd rainforest downpour and watch as the water cascades down streams and bursts into the lily pond. All represent the height of both luxury and value for money. You can expect lots of polished timber, CDs, TVs and double spas on decks (with fantastic views), terracotta tiles in exceptional bathrooms, bamboo blinds, soft robes, good linen and inspiring interior design. Roger and Margaret designed and built each lodge, putting in floodlights so you can sit on your deck at night and look deep into the rainforest. Dinner can be brought to you, or you can eat out or cook your own (each lodge has a fully-equipped kitchen). All this in the heart of a World Heritage National Park, so don't expect to be disturbed! You can climb Mount Warning easily; good paths lead up and the reward is a 360-degree view of rainforest, coast and ocean.

Rooms: 3 lodges each with king doubles and bath and shower.
Price: $245 – $260.
Meals: Continental breakfast included. 2-course dinner by arrangement: $40 p.p.
Directions: Faxed on booking.

Pips Beach Houses

Phil McMaster and Angela James
14 Childe St, Byron Bay 2481
Tel: 02-6685-5400 Fax: 02-6685-5400
Email: pips@nor.com.au Web: www.pipsbyron.com

Lush, thick rainforest, beach-front decks, ocean rollers breaking on the sands and the best sunrise in Australia so bring your alarm clock. Pips is entirely the work of Angela and Phil, who designed and built three beach houses on stilts and then planted their very own two-acre rainforest to wrap them up in. The effect is excellent, creating a great sense of peace and seclusion right on the beachfront. Each house is set back in the rainforest, with a walkway from the front door that leads to a private deck built into the dunes about ten metres above the beach. And it is here that you will loll about all day long, either inside or out. They have built day rooms with day beds so you can fall asleep to the sound of the ocean below. There are boogie boards and surf skis if you want to play in the surf or you can just hang out on the deck and watch the dolphins pass by. Back along the path you'll find your night-time residence, built of marine plywood, so there's a tree-house feel. All are snug and romantic, with hand-painted fabrics, bright colours and lots of sunlight. There are barbecues to cook on, modern art sprinkled about the place and Byron is a twenty-minute walk along the beach. *Whale-watching, swimming, surfing, diving, hang-gliding, sea-kayaking, bush walking, community markets.*

Rooms: 3 beach houses with queen beds for up to 3 adults or for a couple with 2 young kids. All have showers.
Price: $340 – $500. More at Christmas and Easter. Reductions for stays longer than 6 nights.
Meals: Available locally or you cook.
Directions: Leave Pacific Hwy at northern Byron Bay (Ewingsdale Rd) exit. Approx 6km towards Byron, turn left into Kendall. Kendall becomes Childe St. Pips is towards the end on the right.
Postal Address: PO Box 138, Byron Bay 2481.

　Map Number: 2 & 3

Seaview House

Pamela Deylen
146 Lighthouse Rd, Byron Bay 2481
Tel: 02-6685-6468 Fax: 02-6685-6468
Email: pamdseaview@bigpond.com Web: www.seaviewbyron.com

A short walk through rainforest will take you to Byron's famous lighthouse, the most easterly point in Australia. Head west along the beach and a gentle 20-minute stroll will find you in town. If both sound a touch energetic, simply roll down the garden path and land on the beach or stay put on Pam's big, shaded sun deck, sink into the hammock or the day bed and gaze out to sea. From June to October you might well get a whale show to accompany your sundowners. Friends of ours stayed here and couldn't speak highly enough of Pam or her pretty house: typically generous Aussie hospitality, every little comfort thought of and huge breakfasts that include freshly-squeezed juice, home-made muffins and the full cooked works. Bedrooms are big and cool, with tiled floors, fans, air-con, cotton sheets, fresh flowers and spotless shower rooms; the two lower rooms have their own private decks. There's a barbecue if you want to cook for yourselves or you can leave it to Pam and she'll whisk you up something delicious. You can fall asleep to the sound of breaking waves, and sunrise (at about 5.30 a.m.) is spectacular (apparently).

Rooms: 3 queens, 1 with spa bath and shower above, 2 with en-suite shower.
Price: $250 – $300. Singles $180 – $220.
Meals: Full breakfast included. 3-course dinners by arrangement: $40 – $45 p.p.
Directions: In the centre of Byron Bay, pick up and follow signs to lighthouse. At the Captain Cook car park, turn right into Lee Lane. Up hill 100 metres and house signed on left.

New South Wales

Cory's on Cooper

Alan Scott and Alison Cory
21 Cooper Street, Byron Bay 2481
Tel: 02-6685-7834 Fax: 02-6685-7834
Email: corys@mullum.com.au Web: www.corys.com.au

The second-oldest of Byron's big houses, Cory's is a study in relaxed, turn-of-the-century elegance. Although just two minutes' walk to Byron's Tallow Beach, this acre of property i secluded and quiet and perfect for lounging. The garden has more than 200 palm trees, a beautifu dark swimming pool (night swimming very popular in summer) and a beachy covered cabana Unsurprisingly, this is where guests tend to congregate. The house is in fabulous condition, bu Alan is a hard taskmaster and was on the point of re-painting when I visited. Downstairs, 14-foo metal-pressed ceilings and pale yellow hallways compliment rich wooden floors, warm rugs and pictures of Byron by young local photographers. The lounge is cosier and greener, with books music and TV. Large, pale bedrooms have crisp sheets, some antique wooden furniture and flashes of colour, while the master suite has air-con, a double bath and a chimney rising up through the floor. Alan is from the school of very relaxed hosting. He never trained as a cook yet produce exotic breakfasts – the likes of corn and coriander fritters with mango chutney and bacon o buttermilk pancakes with caramelised plums – usually served out on the wooden deck. *15-minute walk to town centre. 2 mins by car.*

Rooms: 4: 2 kings and 2 queens. All have en-suite bathrooms: 1 with double bath and shower; 1 with single bath and shower; 1 with bath/shower; 1 with shower.
Price: $225 – $295 ($350 in high season). Special deals in winter (3 nights for price of 2).
Meals: Full breakfast included.
Directions: From south, leave Pacific Hwy at Ballina and take coast road to Byron. Cooper St is 700m after golf course on R. From north, head through Byron towards Ballina on Jonson St. Cooper St is 5th rd on L after roundabout.

25

Map Number: 2 &

Hume's Hovell Fine B&B

Peter and Suzanne Hume

333 Dalwood Rd, Alstonville 2477
Tel: 02-6629-5371 Fax: 02-6629-5471
Email: stay@humes-hovell.com Web: www.bed-and-breakfast.com.au

I left Peter and Suzanne with perhaps the world's finest jar of macadamia nut chocolate spread stashed in my luggage. This chocolate spread is the culmination of their departure from Sydney 30 years ago. After various careers they ended up going completely nuts (sorry), planting 3000 macadamia trees on their farm. They have a small processing factory on the property and I wandered down with Peter after breakfast as the birds competed to impress me with their song. The farmstead is a large bungalow set around a swimming pool, with two enormous guest suites at either end. These have high ceilings, huge beds, TV, videos, hi-fi, sofas and magazines, and the Plantation suite has a spa in a separate room that looks out over the camellias. There's also a floodlit tennis court. Breakfast included orange juice squeezed from oranges picked that very morning, eggs from their own hens and kumquat jam from their own trees. I ate on the terrace outside my room, but you can choose the pavilion by the pool, which has wooden blinds on all sides. The Humes will often do dinners here and a charcoal brazier keeps you warm if necessary. And rest assured, it's a pun not a hovel. The property is named after two explorers who explored Australia in the early 19th century, Messrs Hume (an ancestor of Peter's) and Hovell. *45 minutes to Byron Bay.*

Rooms: 2: 1 king with en-suite shower; 1 king/twin, en-suite dbl spa and en-suite shower room.
Price: $165 – $230. Singles $130. Extra person from $20. Min stay of 5 nights at Christmas.
Meals: Full breakfast included. Dinner $35 – $60 p.p. depending on what you have (BYO). Complimentary pre-dinner drinks and savouries.
Directions: Follow signs to Alstonville off Pacific Hwy. In Alstonville, go straight through roundabout, then first left towards Wardell. After 5.5km turn right into Dalwood Rd. House is 3km on the left (sign at gates).

Map Number: 2 & 3

The Waterside

Christof and Gabrielle Meyer

80 Tiki Rd, Coffs Harbour 2450
Tel: 02-6653-7388
Fax: 02-6653-7300
Email: holidays@waterside.com.au
Web: www.waterside.com.au

If you cross the garden bridge over the estuary and stroll for fifteen minutes through the national park, you will happen upon six miles of golden sand. The beach is accessible only by foot, so don't expect company… well, not the human kind at least, although dolphins sometimes play in the surf and from May to October whales pass by. If the sea doesn't appeal, try swimming in the creek that bounds the property on two sides. And if that still seems a mite too energetic, stay put at the house and fall asleep in steamer chairs down by the pool. It is very peaceful here. The house is full of an eclectic mix of items picked up by Christof and Gabrielle during lives well lived, and bedrooms have French windows that lead out to a private terrace or balcony, videos, ceiling fans, hand-made rugs, good linen and bath robes. Mine was full of gnarled wood which a local furniture-maker had conjured into headboard, table, sink-surround and mirror frame. The Meyers used to run a restaurant in Sydney and breakfast is, predictably, a proper feast; carrot, apple-ginger juice, orange and mint salad, home-made breads, and pancetta, fresh asparagus and poached egg on an English muffin kept me supremely contented. *In-house beauty treatments, pet porpoise pool, botanic gardens, gold mine tours, white-water rafting, rainforests.*

Rooms: 4: 1 king with en-suite shower; 3 queens, 1 en-suite spa/shower, 1 en-suite bath/shower, 1 en-suite shower.
Price: $165 – $260. Singles $109 – $220. Packages available.
Meals: 3-course breakfast included.
Directions: Travel north through Coffs Harbour. About 11km past the 'Big Banana', turn right off Pacific Highway directly opposite brown sign 'Coffs Harbour Zoo – 500m'. Continue to end of drive and signed.

Monticello Countryhouse

Maryanne Murray
11 Sunset Ridge Drive, Bellingen 2454
Tel: 02-6655-1559 Fax: 02-6655-1559
Email: info@monticello.com.au Web: www.monticello.com.au

So there you are, venturing through the quiet streets of Bellingen. You step nimbly through Maryanne's front door, smiling happily at the prospect of this town B&B. On you go, through the sitting-room, admiring the antiques, chatting to Maryanne. And then you stop. Because as you move onto the verandah, you realise that Bellingen was just a mirage, a theatrical illusion. The scene that confronts you is pure pastoral symphony and the town is nowhere to be seen. The garden swoops downhill from the verandah and there in front of you is the Bellinger River, dominating a rural tableau of water, woody hills and bush. Breakfast is always served outside on the verandah facing the view because, my dear, you would not want to eat anywhere else. It never really gets cold this far north, but there are heaters if the warmth of a three-course gourmet wake-me-up is not sufficient. The house is only 14 years old but Maryanne wanted to recreate the Federation style and the use of dark woods, pale walls and Victorian furniture achieves this admirably. Both rooms have French doors leading onto the verandah and I preferred the blue one with its splendid, separate bathroom. Bellingen really gets going in August when there is a big jazz festival, but Maryanne, who plays bluegrass banjo, can tell you all about that. *10-minute walk to town centre, 30-minute drive to Coffs Harbour.*

Rooms: 2: 1 king/twin with private bath and shower; 1 double with en-suite shower.
Price: $165 – $200. Singles $125.
Meals: Full breakfast included.
Directions: Coming from the east, turn right at the Post Office in Bellingen and go over the bridge. Turn left at the roundabout into Wheatley then go right into Sunset Ridge Drive. House is on the left.

CasaBelle Country House

Fritz and Suzanne Dimmlich
90 Gleniffer Rd, Bellingen 2454
Tel: 02-6655-9311 Fax: 02-6655-0166
Email: casabelle@bigpond.com Web: www.casabelle.com
Cell: 0427-550-155

Bellingen is a small, thriving, artistic community, full of galleries and coffee shops, set in one of th most beautiful river valleys in Australia. And just across its wide and gracious river, far enoug down the road to be described as 'properly rural', Suzanne and Fritz live on a hill with high view across lush cattle-grazing country to the distant mountains of the Dorrigo National Park. We sa on the verandah watching a red sunset, as Fritz explained how he had built his Tuscan-style retrea CasaBelle is architecturally stunning and has a gentle, relaxing feel with lots of open space. Yo flow effortlessly through it, moving from pretty garden to huge sitting-room and on to th cloistered courtyard, off which the large, airy bedrooms are found. The rooms are full of bust ethnic pots and eye-catching objects such as the Indian ox-wagon-cum-coffee-table. Much Suzanne's work and far better than she would ever let you believe! Elsewhere: terracotta-tile floors and coir matting, oil-burning candles, bowls of fruit, gilt-framed mirrors, fresh flowers, ol rugs, bath salts and an easy-going atmosphere. Breakfast is a feast and goes on until noon, so leav your alarm clock at home. There's a forest at the back of the garden too. *Beautiful, unspoile beaches and the Dorrigo rainforests (full of waterfalls) really close by; white-water rafting, scuba-divin in the marine park or whale-watching.*

Rooms: 3: 2 doubles with en/s spa bathrooms, 1 twin/double with en/s shower.
Price: $195 – $225. Singles from $185.
Meals: Full breakfast included and served till noon. Other meals available locally in Bellingen. Candlelit late suppers ($40 p.p.) and picnics ($35 p.p.) on request.
Directions: In Bellingen turn down road by Post Office to roundabout, turn left, continue along this road as it curves sharply. At bottom of curve turn right into CasaBelle. Just 2km from PO.

Map Number:

Telegraph Retreat

Robyn and Ian Whitehead
126 Federation Way, Telegraph Point, via Port Macquarie 2441
Tel: 02-6585-0670 Fax: 02-6585-0671
Email: info@telegraphretreat.com.au Web: www.telegraphretreat.com.au
Cell: 0411-752-764

Another impossibly lovely hideaway with views through the odd shimmering gum tree back towards the rainforest. Robyn and Ian moved here from Melbourne and have made a real family home for themselves – a vegetable garden that produces much for the table, peacocks and geese that you can feed by hand and a heated swimming pool. They live next door to the main federation-style cottage and are on hand to whisk you up a delicious supper and drop freshly baked bread off at your door. This cottage is pristine: wicker chairs out on the verandah; polished wood floors, high ceilings and cool, crisp, contemporary design within. It can easily sleep eight and has ceiling fans and a huge shower. Couples may prefer the new cottages, situated in privacy 200 metres back from the house. These are country casual, open-plan and woody, with white walls, blue or green trim, gingham blinds and hammocks. All the cottages have wood-burners, private spa pools, reverse-cycle air-con, TVs, videos and CD players. Around you is peace and quiet, with parrots, kangaroos, the occasional platypus and a resident kookaburra (did I say peace and quiet?) for company. Robyn and Ian are very much hands-on owners and will talk you through where to swim, where to walk and much more. *On-site aromatherapy massage suite, horse-riding, fishing, bush walks, boat trips, galleries, cafés, restaurants all close by.*

Rooms: 3 cottages: 1 with 1 qn, 1 kg/tw, 2 sgl sofa-beds, 1 dbl sofa-bed, 1 bathroom with bath and sh, 2nd loo. 2 with qn, dbl sofa-bed, e/s bath and sh.

Price: Main cott: $250 per night (2-night min) for up to 4 pax. Other cotts: $220/night for 2 pax; $180 if 2 nights or more. Extra adult $25, extra child $15.

Meals: Continental breakfast provisions included. 3-course dinners $45 p.p., or supper provisions available. Picnic/barbecue hampers from $22.

Directions: 4 hours N of Sydney, 15 mins N of Port Macquarie. Follow "Telegraph Retreat" signs, take 1st turn N of Wilson River into Rollands Plains Rd, then 1st left into Cooperabung Dr. After 4km L into Federation Way."TR" 1.2km.

Map Number: 3

Toms Creek Retreat

Margaret and Stewart Williams

223 Toms Creek Road, Ellenborough 2446
Tel: 02-6587-4313 Fax: 02-6587-4313
Email: tomscreekretreat@bigpond.com
Web: www.tomscreekretreat.com.au Cell: 0412-199-484

Toms Creek Retreat sits on top of a spur that juts out into the lush greenery of the Hastings Valley near the Oxley Highway. It has a remarkable position, with the land dropping away on three sides eucalypts and rainforest all around. Just as I arrived the mist lifted, in suspiciously timely fashion, c the surrounding hills – I looked for the button in Margaret's hand. The rosellas kept on nibblin on the lawn meanwhile; they had clearly seen such displays before. The Williamses serve up very relaxed, ecologically-friendly experience at Toms Creek Retreat. The bottom of the propert borders the Ellenborough River, where there is fishing, swimming and platypus-searching. An there are walking trails slashed through the 160 acres; you can walk up to the top of the nearb mountain if indolence is not your thing. The three cottages are very private and perched on the hillside looking down through the trees. With high ceilings they are roomy and light, with kitchens music systems, TVs, videos, books and board games to keep you amused. Margaret and Stewar bought the property from a wood-carver (check out the dining chalet) at the beginning of this yea They're a very friendly couple – big grins and warm handshakes – who can provide meals (wanted) and charm (no choice) in large quantities. *Wallabies, echidnas, possums and more than 5 bird species.*

Rooms: 3 cottages: all have queens with en-suite bath/shower, plus double futons in lounge; one has bunks as well.
Price: $100 – $160. Singles $70 – $100. Extra couple $70, extra adult $40, extra child (3 – 15) $30
Meals: Full breakfast $10 p.p. – either hamper provided or cooked and served in dining chalet. Dinner: $30 p.p for 2 courses, $40 for 3 courses.
Directions: Turn west off the Pacific Hwy near Port Macquarie. Head along Oxley Hwy to Ellenborough. Left in Ellenborough (signed Toms Creek). 2km takes you to the retreat.

Benbellen Country Retreat

Peter Wildblood and Sherry Stumm
Cherry Tree Lane, Hannam Vale 2443
Tel: 02-6556-7788 Fax: 02-6556-7778
Email: peter@benbellen.com.au Web: www.bbfarmstay.com.au

Not many know of Hannam Vale, although you may often pass the turn on the Pacific Highway. I am doing my bit, I suppose, to let the cat out of the bag. Peter and Sherry also fell for the green valleys, woods, streams, dairy farms and rollercoasting country lanes and I am not the first, I feel sure, to have been reminded of England. The peak of South Brother seals off the valley and adds a touch of majesty. Benbellen is a stilted Queenslander-style home which catches every breeze, and from the high verandah Peter and Sherry can keep an eye on their animals: the friesians in the top paddock beyond the lotus-fringed dam, the alpacas (now 14 strong), the chickens, the guinea fowl, the Indian runner ducks and their twin sheep dogs Tom and Jerry. On the inside, the house is dominated by a wide, open-plan living area with two alcoves for more intimate socialising and a central dining table where masterpieces are laid out for undeserving guests. Absolutely everything I ate at Benbellen was not just good but memorable – and very healthy too. Both Sherry and Peter are published authors and the house bulges with books. Self-contained Penlan Cottage is 10km down the road, equally stylish with great views. *Take a boat, swim or fish for bass and warm-water rainbow trout; early morning walks; health weekends once a month.*

Rooms: 3: all queens with en-suite shower.
Price: $175 (1 night), $145 (2 or more nights). Singles $135 (1 night), $110 (2 or more nights).
Meals: Breakfast included. Dinner $35 for 3 courses including wine.
Directions: From Pacific Hwy north past Taree for 29km to Moorland. Turn left into Hannam Vale Rd and through village of Hannam Vale. Straight ahead on Waitui Road and then right into Cherry Tree Lane to the end.
Postal Address: PO Box 58, Coopernook 2426.

Jenkins Street Guest House

Judy Howarth
85 Jenkins St, Nundle 2340
Tel: 02-6769-3239 Fax: 02-6769-3239
Email: ghnundle@northnet.com.au Web: www.nundle.info

You can stand safely in hilly Nundle and watch the herds of food writers as they migrate from Sydney to the Jenkins Street Guest House for the best grazing. Much fuss is rightly made, too, of the elegance and stylish simplicity of this converted bank (1936): polished wood floors and damask linen in bedrooms, sleek, chic bathrooms… and the downstairs restaurant (just thirty covers) smells as enticing as it looks. But I was even more impressed by the natural way you are welcomed in and how friendly and lively the place is. Judy outdoes her own ideal of a guest house, receiving guests as old friends and getting in amongst it with the gardening. In winter, snow settles on the highest ground surrounding Nundle and guests huddle round log fires after bracing walks. In summer, there is the garden, a channel of smooth lawn flanked by trees, which runs steeply down into a gully. This is the venue for pre-dinner drinks and, now and then, string quartets play on fine evenings. The guest house also owns a woollen mill in town, which you can visit, and a farm two kilometres down the road, available to all overnighting guests. Attractions include Jake the tame eastern grey kangaroo, historic gardens laid out in the late 1800s, a yabbie farm and forest walks. What *don't* they have?

Rooms: 6: 5 in the house: 1 with en-suite shower; 2 with en-suite bath; 2 sharing 1 shower. Also 1 cottage with en-suite shower.
Price: $110 – $160 B&B.
Meals: Full breakfast included. Dinners à la carte in the restaurant. Lunches at weekends (mains roughly $18 – $20). Licensed for alcohol.
Directions: House in centre of Nundle.

Map Number: 3 &

Tranquil Vale Vineyard

Phil and Lucy Griffiths
325 Pywells Road, Luskintyre, Hunter Valley 2321
Tel: 02-4930-6100 Fax: 02-4930-6105
Email: stay@tranquilvale.com.au Web: www.tranquilvale.com.au

The Griffithses have a reputation in this northern part of the Hunter Valley as the couple who bought their beautiful property without seeing it. And I for one (of many) was mightily impressed by both bravura and result. While living in England they saw an ad for some land, sent a Sydney friend up to have a look and, on receiving a glowing report, they bought the place. An old dairy farm became a new vineyard and, *voilà*, Tranquil Vale was born. They took over full-time in 1998 and, after studying viticulture locally, now produce shiraz, sémillon and chardonnay. Guests are offered a tasting on arrival and can ask all the wine questions they feel they should already know the answers to, without embarrassment. It's that kind of a place. Both Phil and Lucy were foreign exchange traders in previous lives, but I suspect their people skills were wasted. Phil juggled wine-tasters, vine grafters, budders, me and the school run and dropped nothing. Three modern guest cottages look out over the vines to the hills beyond, with shrubbery all around them. There are comforts ancient (fire, view) and modern (TV, video, music) and a separate BBQ area if the restaurants of the Hunter Valley don't tempt you. And if you want to feel you've earned all this cosseting, punish yourself in the 15-metre pool, floodlit tennis court and fully-equipped gym.

Rooms: 3 cottages: each has one king/twin room, one double room, shower room, sitting-room, dining area and kitchen.
Price: $575 per cottage for two nights at the weekend. $220 per night during the week. Specials available for longer stays.
Meals: Full breakfast pack included for first morning. BBQ packs available for $18 p.p.
Directions: From Sydney: take Freeway towards Newcastle then turn along New England Hwy through Maitland. 12km after Maitland turn R to Windermere/Luskintyre. L to Luskintyre over bdge. 3km to T-jct and turn L. "TV" is 2nd property on R.

Lillians on Lovedale

Bill and Sally Sneddon

Lovedale Road, Lovedale, Hunter Valley 2320
Tel: 02-4990-6958 Fax: 02-4990-1714
Email: info@lillians.com.au Web: www.lillians.com.au
Cell: 040-868-1552

I fear this is one of those places, in one of those areas, where you could quite easily wake up one morning and realise you were meant to be back at work three days previously. It's lovely from the word go, an enchanting cottage in the middle of the Hunter Valley, a place to relax and snooze and select a winery or five to visit. The living area is floored in spotted gum (much darker and richer than pine), with sunlight or spotlight reflecting off pale walls, while sofa and armchairs and open fireplace all murmur 'stay'. There's a fabulous kitchen (fridge, oven, dishwasher, microwave) that looks out into the bush, a worktop made from an old school woodwork bench and a dining table made from a barn door. Bedrooms are spotless and simply decorated in whites and taupe and one bathroom has a spa. The cottage sits on 25 acres of what was originally an old dairy farm and all is yours to explore. You may not meet the Sneddons (they're very nice, if you do!), but you could well bump into Bill at the nearby Allandale Winery, where you pick up the keys – he's the winemaker there. Breakfast provisions are supplied each day for you to 'do a Jamie': bacon, eggs, orange juice, Turkish or damper bread, muesli, cereal etc.

Rooms: 1 cottage with 2 bedrooms (king/twin and queen), 1 with en-suite shower, 1 with separate spa and shower.
Price: $165 for one couple midweek. $308 for 2 couples. Weekends: $682 – $700 for 1 or 2 couples for 2 nights. Discounts for 3 or more nights.
Meals: Full breakfast provisions included.
Directions: Head north from Cessnock on Allandale Road. Before you reach the airport, turn right onto Lovedale Road at the golf course. Go past Allandale Winery and Lillians is a bit further up on the right.
Postal Address: c/o Allandale Winery, Lovedale Road, Lovedale 2320.

Map Number: 3 &

Fernwood Terrace Bed & Breakfast

Jim and Maria Young
16 Ravenshaw St, The Junction, Newcastle 2291
Tel: 02-4969-2912 Fax: 02-4969-2567
Email: comestay@fernwoodbandb.com Web: www.fernwoodbandb.com
Cell: 0416-220-500

Maria is one of those B&B owners who can't quite believe that what they do is actually a job. "I love it with a passion!" she declares of her 'business' in Newcastle's Junction suburb. This 1875 terrace house was the family home, but now bursts with the embodiment of that passion: forests of plants, cookies in jars, cakes on trays, rugs on floors and mounds of cushions in the bedrooms. At the heart of it all is the enormous kitchen where Maria struts her stuff and I will go to my grave regretting that I missed breakfast. Highlights include eight or nine (!) different types of muesli from as far away as Byron Bay and the Blue Mountains, one of them soaked overnight in apple juice and covered in berries. Other offerings include porridge with cinnamon apples, poached egg on lime spinach, poached pear in saffron. You can digest your food and the news in one of the sitting areas inside (wood-stoves, books, magazines and cable TV ensure you feel no rush to stand up again); or outside in the small central courtyard. Personally, I would choose the converted bath in the shady front garden. An excellent city B&B. *Walking distance to beaches (superb surfing) and restaurants. 40 mins to Hunter Valley vineyards. Nature reserves, golfing nearby.*

Rooms: 3: 1 queen, 1 double, 1 twin; 1 en-suite spa/shower, 1 en-suite shower, 1 private shower.
Price: $149 – $175. Singles $99 – $105.
Meals: Full breakfast included.
Directions: Ask when booking.

Mountain Valley Roo-treat

John and Jolieske Medcalf
'Flatlands', Clandulla 2848
Tel: 02-6379-4318 Fax: 02-6379-6180
Email: rootreat@winsoft.net.au
Cell: 0429-794-318

You just won't have enough eyes to cope with your first impressions at Mountain Valley. You brea out of the trees after a few kilometres of gravel road (I saw rosellas, a fox and a tortoise en route onto clear ground collared by forested hills on three sides. An impossibly idyllic 1830s stone an corrugated-iron homestead faces towards the fourth point of the compass, a wide valley tha plunges down from the garden and ranges forth for miles and miles. The setting is not one inc short of exquisite. Closer to home, you are surrounded by green lawns, flowers, butterflies, bird visiting kangaroos, fruit trees… with birdsong and the swish of air moving through gum leaves fc musical accompaniment. There is a swimming pool with sensational views and a boating lak where mobs of kangaroos and the odd wombat come to drink at dusk. By day, explorers will b out in the hills or peering into the house's rickety outbuildings. Inside, this is the perfect rusti cottage, with wood floors, open fires, fresh flowers, faded rugs, brass beds, antiques, Aborigin art works and an old wooden kitchen a-clatter with hanging pots and pans. John and Joliesk ('Yoleeska') live further up the mountain and come down to cook the breakfast and welcome the guests to heaven. You can visit the Mudgee wineries from here, but for me this is far too preciou a find to waste a minute of my time somewhere else.

Rooms: 1 cottage with 3 bedrooms sharing 2 bathrooms (1 with bath/shower and 1 with shower). Also one outdoor shower.
Price: $125 – $135. Singles $80 – $90.
Meals: Full breakfast included and served until any time. Dinners $85 (per couple) for 3 courses including a bottle of local wine.
Directions: Mountain Valley Roo-treat is near Rylstone, near Mudgee, 3 hours from Sydney – a map will be faxed to you when you book. 'Flatlands' is the postal address.

Map Number: 3 &

Bed of Roses

Dee and Rob Napier

Kyalla Park, Forbes Rd, Orange
2800
Tel: 02-6362-6946
Fax: 02-6361-7492
Email:
dee_napier@bigfoot.com
Web: www.bedofroses.net.au

The Black Sheep Inn needs to be seen to be believed! Dee has cunningly crossed a modern guest house with an original Aussie shearing shed, complete (and I mean complete!) with its original 1920s machinery. The result? Aussie farm chic! Sheep were herded into this massive corrugated-iron shed to catching pens on one side, now the sitting-room with sofas surrounding a cast-iron wood-burner. The sitting-room is accessed through swing doors (still shiny with use) where sheep were dragged out for shearing under the red Sunbeam machines (left as last used). Wool was thrown onto the slatted wool table (now glass-topped and seating twenty) for classing and packed into the towering 18-ft tall, box wool-press. Curling down the shed, old spray pipes in the roof have been converted into halogen lighting above acres of scrubbed wooden floorboards. Wide windows allow stunning views of the surrounding fields. Bedrooms are in exquisite contrast, sophisticated and glamorous with antiques, black and silver carpets and silver mohair blankets covering deep beds. For true B&B, opt for Dee's beautiful house surrounded by acres of lawns, lavender, hedges and lily ponds and be spoiled by her directly. Or there's the privacy of Whispering Moon Cottage, a self-catering option with bright furnishings, a contemporary feel and a deck overlooking the countryside. Wherever you stay will be an outstanding experience.

Rooms: 3 houses. Whispering Moon: 2 queens, 1 en/s bath, 1 en/s shr. Homestead: 3 queens, 2 en/s shr, 1 en/s bath. Black Sheep Inn: 5 queen, 4 en/s shr, 1 en/s bath.
Price: $175 – $225. Min 2-night stay at weekends.
Meals: Full breakfast provided at the Homestead and Black Sheep Inn. Gourmet hamper breakfasts are left for you in Whispering Moon.
Directions: From Orange take the Forbes Road (turn off the Mitchell Hwy at West Orange Motors) and after 6.5km turn left onto Heifer Station Lane. 1st left for the Homestead and Black Sheep Inn; 3rd left for Whispering Moon.

Map Number: 4

Collits' Inn

Cyrillia van der Merwe (manager), Laurent Deslandes (chef) and Christine Stewart (owner)
Hartley Vale Road, Hartley Vale 2790
Tel: 02-6355-2072 Fax: 02-6355-2073
Email: info@collitsinn.com.au Web: www.collitsinn.com.au

An early guest, Captain W. Dumaresq, was smitten by Collits' Inn and wrote in 1827: "It beautiful and picturesque, warm, comfortable and commodious on the inside." The captain's view is no less true today. The inn has stood beneath Mount York in kangaroo-filled Hartley Vale since 1823, when it was established by a former convict. One of the oldest inns in the Blue Mountains three governors stayed there between 1823 and 1832. Christine rescued the inn from dereliction in 2001 and rebuilt it to a degree of luxury beyond the most feverish imaginings of Captain Dumaresq. The restoration remained faithful to the building's origins wherever possible with the same duck pond and stone stables nearby, bowed walls, low ceilings and origin fireplaces in both dining-rooms. Antique oak benches and tables maintain the sense of romance and antiquity. The inn also concentrates on its bedrooms and cooking… and excels at every turn Laurent spent 10 years as a chef in Paris and then worked at one of the most popular French restaurants in Sydney; as a result Collits' Inn has been awarded two Best Restaurant awards. Enjoy your breakfast of rice pudding, croissants and baguettes, not necessarily in that order, while watching the roos mow the lawn. *The inn has a history room, a shop and a pioneer cemetery behind. There are fascinating walks down old roads that once led to the inn. Jenolan Caves nearby.*

Rooms: 5: 1 king, en/s sh & bath, 1 queen en/s sh & b, 1 twin with private sh. The Stables (s/c): 2 dbls sharing bath & sh. Brown House (s/c): 2 dbl & 2 sgls.
Price: $180 – $225 per weekend night. 10% off for 2nd night or weekdays. The Stables $500 per 2-night weekend, Brown House $400.
Meals: Restaurant open Thurs to Mon for evening meals and for lunch at weekends. Courses about $16 entrée, $28 main, $13 dessert. Fully licensed.
Directions: From Sydney take M1/Gt Western Hwy towards Mt Victoria. Go down Victoria Pass. Just past Little Hartley take 2nd road on right, Browns Gap Rd – stay on the tarmac. At T-junction turn right and go 2km. Collits' is on right.

Map Number: 3 &

Kanimbla View Environmental Retreat

Hilary Hughes and Gary Werskey
113 Shipley Road, Blackheath 2785
Tel: 02-4787-8985 Fax: 02-4787-6665
Email: kanimbla@lisp.com.au Web: www.kanimbla.com

Hilary has built two stunning, fully-screened cottages which are as ecological as you can imagine, with solar power, furniture made from trees felled on the surrounding land (and only felled to make way for more indigenous flora) and immensely tall sash windows salvaged from a demolition in Sydney. The interiors have a pleasantly chic, ethnic feel to them – with Indonesian ikat fabric on cushions and curtains – the walls and floors are all ochres and reds and painted with natural paints. The central space is a split-level kitchen/sitting-room with a wood-burning stove and books and games. You will discover the pleasures of the (odourless) rota-loo dry-composting toilets and marvel at the peace and quiet broken only by the occasional lyre bird or king parrot. Hilary is an expert guide and offers all guests a nature tour on the property where she will point out the intricacies of the Australian bush and show you the spectacular viewpoints at Kanimbla. As you sit drinking your organic coffee or perhaps as you slip between your natural hemp sheets, you too will dream of transforming your home into an ecological paradise – it just *looks* so easy. *Two nights minimum stay. Picnicking at one of the viewpoints, tennis, table tennis, large spa bath, canyoning, horse-riding... and all the walks the Blue Mountains have to offer.*

Rooms: 2 cottages with 2 kings/twins and 1 double (with extra single bed), sharing 2 shower-rooms, plus kitchen and sitting-room.
Price: Weeknights: $170 1-2 people, $260 4 people, $330 6 people. W-ends/public holidays: $340 4 people, $400 5 people, $450 6 people. All prices per night. 2-night min stay.
Meals: Breakfast basket can be provided on the first morning for an additional $10 p.p. Otherwise, self-catering and excellent restaurants nearby.
Directions: In Blackheath cross the railway and turn first left into Station St, then first right into Shipley Rd for 2.5km. Kanimbla View on your right.
Postal Address: PO Box 252, Blackheath 2785.

Map Number: 3 & 4

Across the Waters Dangar Island

Helen and Jim Jones

49 Grantham Crescent, Dangar Island 2083
Tel: 02-9985-8599 Fax: 02-9985-7574
Email: info@acrossthewaters.aust.com Web: www.acrossthewaters.com.au
Cell: 0414-430-537

As I wandered along the tree-shaded paths of this small island – no cars and hardly any peopl (population 150) – I felt that I had been magicked away to a Polynesian paradise. Yet you'r officially still in Sydney, a laughable thought. And nowhere is this thought more laughable than a Across the Waters, a stunning collection of cottages and guest rooms in the Joneses' own beac house. Wonderful waterfront locations plus inspired design equals Greenwood nirvana. On cottage – cool whites and wood floors spiced with modern art and statuettes – juts out over th water down by the ferry wharf and you can pretty much fish from the bed. It is quite – and I us this word under advisement – divine. The main house is on the beach side of the island (5 mir walk), surrounded and refreshed by ebullient plants, with a dazzling swimming pool that melts int its tropical surrounds. Supper, styled Australian new food cuisine, is usually served out here b candlelight, looking over Bradley's Beach towards the sea and the woody islands and headland all around; but you can be served in your cottage too. If staying in the house, I suggest you splas out a bit further and choose the downstairs suite. "We've beached it up a bit," says Helen. It glorious. But then so is everything here. This *must* be the ultimate Sydney escape.

Rooms: 5 cottages: 1 has 3 bedrooms, 2 bathrooms; 3 have 2 beds, 1 bath; 1 has 1 bed, 1 bath. 2 rooms in main house: both queens, 1 e/s spa & shower, 1 e/s shower.
Price: $1180 – $1380 per couple per weekend (2 nights). Midweek from $500 per couple per night. Self-catering rates available for the cottages.
Meals: Full breakfast and three-course dinner included. Bring your own wine.
Directions: From Sydney; take Pacific Hwy north to the F3. Exit freeway after crossing Hawkesbury River bridge. Follow signs to Brooklyn. In Brooklyn go to ferry wharf. Park and get ferry to Dangar Island. Ask Helen for ferry details.

Kathryns on Queen

Kathryn Bruderlin
20 Queen St, Woollahra, Sydney 2025
Tel: 02-9327-4535 Fax: 02-9327-4535
Email: info@kathryns.com.au Web: www.kathryns.com.au

You may not be greeted by Kathryn herself when you pull up to her smart Paddington terrace house, as her friends enjoy running it so much for her when she's away, but you'll know if she's there from her cheery welcome. With a keen eye for precious properties, Kathryn bought the run-down terrace four years ago and put much work into restoring it to its present and former splendour. Built in 1888, the house is an excellent example of Italianate Victorian architecture, with its cast-iron Sydney lace, double-height ceilings, detailed plasterwork and tiled hallway. Above the door, the stained glass announces "Tara", the town in Ireland where the builder came from. Kathryn has created an elegant European feel, with airy, sun-bathed rooms (at least they were sun-bathed when I visited) filled with pale, antique furniture. Or what she likes to call "shabby chic". Prize amongst these must be the 19th-century, French, washed-wood bed in La Grande bedroom. The first-floor rooms both have large windows and balconies (La Grande's faces Queen Street; La Petite's the rear courtyard garden with its espaliered camellias). But it is the top floor bedroom, Le Attic, of which Kathryn is most proud, as it best shows off her enterprising use of the natural features of the building. The dinky en-suite bathroom built around the chimney breast is a treat! *Heart of fashionable Paddington with plethora of shops, restaurants and bars.*

Rooms: 3: 1 double and 1 queen sharing shower and bath; 1 long queen with en-suite shower.
Price: $150 – $190.
Meals: Full breakfast included. Surfeit of leading restaurants nearby.
Directions: Queen St is just off Oxford St in Woollahra, adjoining Paddington, but a map can be faxed with more details.

Marshalls of Paddington

David and Donna Marshall
73 Goodhope St, Paddington, Sydney 2021
Tel: 02-9361-6217 Fax: 02-9361-6986
Email: dmarsh@zipworld.com.au Web: www.marshallsbnb.net

Booking in at Marshalls means winning the keys to your very own Paddington pad… and much more besides. You get the run of the place, your own front door and large sitting-room, complete with flat-screen telly, gas fire, loads of CDs (Australian jazz a Marshall obsession) and books, video-player, music system, deep, jump-on-me sofas and armchairs. And upstairs a beautiful, fresh-feeling double bedroom, a shower-room and another single bedroom that doubles as a dressing room. Double doors open from the bedroom to the balcony for evening snifters before you climb the street to eat at Fiveways. If you've got the oomph, the restaurant strips of Darlinghurst and Oxford Street are very close too. Donna and David, meanwhile, look after you far better than you deserve! They enjoy a chat if you're up for it and, if the opportunity arises during your stay, sailing can be organised on their yacht, the *Free Spirit*; or David will show you round the eastern suburb coast and point you towards the ferry to return to Circular Quay. A hearty cooked breakfast includes freshly-squeezed orange juice, seasonal fruits, yoghurt, home-made bread and plunger coffee. But there are no end of little extras such as fresh fruit cake, flowers, bathrobes, electric blankets…. All this for the price is amazing.

Rooms: 1 double and 1 single sharing a shower. Single party bookings only.
Price: $150. $60 for an extra adult.
Meals: Full breakfast included. A couple of minutes from Fiveways and 5 minutes from Oxford Street which are both covered in restaurants.
Directions: Ask when booking or see map on web site.

The Chelsea

Stephen Smith (manager)

49 Womerah Ave, Darlinghurst, Sydney 2010
Tel: 02-9380-5994 Fax: 02-9332-2491
Email: xchelsea@ozemail.com.au Web: www.chelsea.citysearch.com.au

Various magazines, various designers and pretty much every person who's walked through the front door have congratulated Stephen on what he's achieved at The Chelsea. The Greenwood Guides followed suit. This is a beautiful place, created from 1870s terraced houses in a quiet Darlinghurst road. We visited on a March day when the rest of Sydney was heating up, but The Chelsea is a place where there always seems to be a breeze to soothe fevered brows. Stephen has created a light-filled temple to good taste, a seamless collection of bright, stylish, yet immensely liveable spaces. Light pours in through skylights and French windows onto yellow walls. The downstairs area is floored in warm Italian tiles and drifts into a courtyard bursting with flowers, lillipilli trees and pond. Bedrooms are a joy – either dreamily French provincial or sleekly contemporary. All have sisal rugs, damask linen and big mirrors, and most have doors opening onto conservatory, courtyard or private balcony looking over Darlinghurst. Don't get the wrong impression though: The Chelsea is as informal as it is stylish. Guests can help themselves to the fridge, take wee Lewis for a walk or just sit in courtyard or lounge and chat to Stephen about what to do if they can be persuaded out of the house.

Rooms: 13: 2 kings, 3 'deluxe' queens, 4 queens, all with en-suite shower; 4 singles sharing 2 showers.
Price: $143 – $180. Singles $93.50 – $100.
Meals: Continental breakfast included.
Directions: Situated just off Liverpool Street in Darlinghurst. Map on web site.

Tricketts

Liz Trickett

270 Glebe Point Rd, Glebe, Sydney 2037
Tel: 02-9552-1141 Fax: 02-9692-9462
Email: trickettsbandb@hotmail.com Web: www.tricketts.com.au

After 25 years restoring old houses (mainly in England and Italy), Liz was looking for a Sydney building with the appropriate age, grace and grandeur to house her fine collections of English and Australian antique furniture, her Persian rugs, her baby grand piano et al. And this stunning, almost baronial, Victorian mansion more than fits the bill, complete with ballroom for the baby grand, ceiling picked out in gold leaf. Everywhere you look there is something to admire: parquet flooring, original stained glass, beautiful 1880s tessellated tiles in the hall. Liz not only generously shares her possessions with her guests, but encourages you to treat the place as home. The kitchen and breakfasting area are open-plan. Make yourself coffee or tea whenever you want (hot water constant in the zip). Continental breakfast is served on the large deck in fine weather and there are plenty of other spaces where you can settle with a book: the marble-topped circular table and chairs on the downstairs verandah or the semi-outdoor first-floor verandah. Beds are 'posturepedic', showers have been cunningly incorporated into large rooms with modern glass bricks – a room within a room. Tricketts is as comfortable as it is stylish, very central – a bus runs straight past the front door to The Rocks – and there are 95 (!) restaurants on Glebe Point Rd. *Air-conditioning throughout.*

Rooms: 8: 7 house rooms: 5 queen, 1 king and 1 queen/twin, all with en/s showers. 1 garden apartment with en/s shower (where children are welcome).
Price: $176 – $220. Singles $160 – $200. Apartment $198 for two, $250 for three.
Meals: Special Continental breakfast included. 95 restaurants on the same street.
Directions: Ask when booking.

Lofthouse B&B

Leslie and David Bottomley

17 Seaman Street, Greenwich, Sydney 2065
Tel: 02-9437-3316
Fax: 02-9437-3383
Email:
leslie@lofthousebandb.com.au
Web:
www.lofthousebandb.com.au
Cell: 0418-238-058

Could we have found our Superwoman? Leslie bakes bread, makes jam, takes evocative wildlife photos and recently floated her own travel company. And she still finds time to enjoy the ever-changing sunset from her cliff-top balcony. Perched on a wooded hillside, their Queen Anne Federation house is a marriage of sensitive restoration and subtle mod cons. To wit: the parquet-floored bedrooms have guest-controlled piped music; the ornate ceiling masks a fibre-optic lighting system that brings their South African art collection to life. The bedrooms are full of seductive touches, tempting you to linger: a suggestive chaise-longue, a fridge full of free drinks, a guest laundry. There is also a private self-contained apartment with north-facing windows and floral courtyard, an ideal nest from which to observe native wildlife in the garden. At the end of the day you'll doubtless find yourself on the commanding balcony that stretches out from the living-room, suspended above sandstone terraces that cascade down the cliff to a glass-encased lap pool. Don't worry if you haven't the energy to get down there; tomorrow was made for good intentions. Join Leslie and David for a sundowner instead and be carried away by the birdsong and views across the Lane Cove River inlet. *Golf, tennis and 120 restaurants in nearby Lane Cove, $25 pick-up from airport.*

Rooms: 3: 1 double room plus 1 twin room sharing private shower; 1 apartment with queen-size bedroom, en-suite shower, separate kitchen and lounge.
Price: $150 – $200. Singles $10 off room rate.
Meals: Full breakfast included, with home-made breads, jams and yoghurts. Lunch and dinner by request. 3-course dinner: $33 per person.
Directions: A map can be faxed when booking and full directions are available on web site.
Postal Address: PO Box 5086, Greenwich 2065.

101 Addison Road B&B

Jill Caskey
Manly, Sydney 2095
Tel: 02-9977-6216 Fax: 02-9976-6352
Email: jcaskey@bb-manly.com Web: www.bb-manly.com

Houses, like cats, have many lives. During The Depression and WWII many of the houses in Manly were converted into holiday flats and, when renovated, the partition walls were dismantled to reveal perfectly-preserved cedar panelling and Baltic pine floorboards. Jill's sitting-room is an excellent example, with its magnificent concertina wood doors, 400-year-old English blanket box and open fire that cackles away come winter. It's all too tempting to settle in for the afternoon. Jill and her somewhat discerning cat, Puss, are music lovers and encourage visiting musos to strike up on the grand piano or her grandfather's violin which he used to play to any who would listen. Not musical? Delve into a good book. Prize amongst these is her dad's captivating memoir, ending with his journey to Australia from Shropshire in 1924, with its engrossing description of his first view of Manly. For those with more energy, take a bracing walk along the North Head or a swim at Manly beach and return to one of two guest rooms: one with cast-iron fireplace and a long ladder leading up to a lofty artist's studio; the other with iron bed, bulging bookcase and French windows to the verandah, where you can recuperate under the fragrant frangipanis and the floodlit St Patrick's College, nowadays less charmingly known as the International College for Tourism and Hotel Management. The monks have long since gone west.

Rooms: 2 rooms available to a single group. 1 queen-size, 1 double and a spare bed all sharing a bathroom with bath and shower and separate loo.
Price: $130 – $150. Singles $90 – $110.
Meals: Special breakfast included with fresh fruit salad, cereals, yoghurt, breads, home-made preserves and very fresh coffee.
Directions: A map is available on the web site and Jill can arrange airport transfer. Ferries run from Circular Quay to Manly regularly. The trip takes 30 mins.

Little Forest

Ann Carney
Old Hume Highway, Alpine via Mittagong, Southern Highlands 2575
Tel: 02-4889-4229 Fax: 02-4889-4229
Email: annc@hinet.net.au Web: www.highlandsnsw.com.au/littleforest

I could have stumbled upon some idealised landscape from Beatrix Potter so dingly a dell was this! There are creeks and billabongs, melaleucas and ironbarks (reputedly the finest stand in the Southern Highlands), rhododendrons and a field of lavender. And, planted in the middle, the three cottages, bound to the scenery by a cocoon of green vegetation and lovingly watched over by Hector, Ann's 50-year-old donkey. Sometimes self-catering cottages can seem sterile, but these have the happy, lived-in feel of real homes. The largest, Lavender House, was built in the 1870s. Its wooden deck faces a grove of waratahs, while indoors there's a large, wood-floored living area and claw-foot tub. The Studio Cottage next door is the cosiest of the three, made of convict-hewn stone salvaged from the 19th-century inn that once stood on the site. And set slightly apart, The Pottery is covered in flowers and shrubs. A rustic timber building, its insides are entirely sophisticated with handsome white bedrooms and lovely bathrooms. Ann provides innumerable breakfast goodies for the first two days of your stay, including bowls of oranges that you can juice in the machine, bacon, eggs and home-made jam. All cottages have secluded outdoor sitting areas and there is plenty of scope for wandering on the 46 acres. From time to time you can hear trains on the nearby railway, but this never derails the overall atmosphere of peace and seclusion.

Rooms: 3 cottages: 1 with 3 rooms, 2 queens and 1 twin, 1 en-s shower, other 2 rooms share bath and sh; 1 with qu and tw, b and sh; 1 with king/twin and qu, en-s b and sh.
Price: $150 – $220. Extra person from $22 a night.
Meals: Breakfast-making facilities can be provided for first two days.
Directions: Coming from Sydney take the Colo Vale exit off the M5 Expressway. Turn left at the first junction and drive 4.5km. Just before an old railway bridge you will see Little Forest on the left.

Fitzroy Inn

Cosmo and Maria Aloi and Paul and Gai Lovell
26 Ferguson Crescent, Mittagong 2575
Tel: 02-4872-3457 Fax: 02-4871-3451
Email: fitzroyinn@acenet.com.au Web: www.fitzroyinn.com.au

In the late afternoon sun the Fitzroy Inn emits a lazy glow. A child of the mid-1830s, it's a beautiful terracotta-coloured structure, the oldest-surviving NSW inn in its original condition. Under the terms of the first land grant a minimum of £200 *had* to be spent on the building. That wasn't cheap in 1835, so the inn is pretty big. There are two huge rooms upstairs, both deliciously simple, with white tongue-and-groove walls, white linen and gable windows. All six rooms in the main building are simple – the Lovells and Alois are ardent fans of the uncluttered look – all with massive showers and range-topping mattresses and there are four more rooms in the Schoolmaster's Cottage nearby. The Fitzroy was their holiday home, but cometh the hour, cometh the lifestyle change and they decided to return it to its original role. Once you've arrived, you'll search in vain for a reason to leave (ever) because there's a restaurant on site. Cosmo and Gai run this and offer a small, seasonal menu. If there are six or fewer house guests they will often serve breakfast in the main kitchen. Make sure you wander downstairs where there has been much restoration; you can see the original kitchen area and the room for poorer visitors and admire the cell where convicts travelling to Berrima could be kept overnight. It still works, so watch your manners.

Rooms: 10: all queens, 3 can convert to twins; all en-suite (1 spa and shower, 1 bath and shower, 2 bath/shower, 6 shower).
Price: Midweek $170 – $190; weekends $220 – $250. Singles less $20. Dining packages often available.
Meals: Full breakfast included and dinners available à la carte in the restaurant.
Directions: From Sydney, take the first Mittagong exit off the Hume Freeway. After 5km you'll come to a golf course on your right and Ferguson Crescent is first road on the left.
Postal Address: PO Box 199, Mittagong 2575.

Berrima Guest House

Wendy and Michael Roodbeen
Cnr Oxley and Wilkinson Sts, Berrima 2577
Tel: 02-4877-2277 Fax: 02-4877-2345
Email: hillside@hinet.net.au Web: www.berrimaguesthouse.com

The kernel of Berrima Guest House is an 1843 cottage, which has been restored and somehow incorporated into the new building. Its sweet façade, corrugated-iron canopy and even an illuminated stone water well are enclosed to confusing effect in the sunny atrium – a house within a house. The verandah that runs along the front of the new building looks down onto a croquet lawn and it is particularly pleasant to watch others competing ferociously as you nurse a tea or beer. The garden was in its infancy when Simon visited two years ago, but is now flourishing and the magnolias are speeding skywards, aping the tall cypresses and macrocarpa pines which must have been there as long as the old tennis pavilion and stables. The bedrooms are in simple, solid, country style with hefty wooden beds, yellow-washed walls, the odd green plant or original fireplace, electric blankets for winter, ceiling fans for summer and three rooms have their own small gravel courtyard and access. Bathrooms are very white with terracotta-tiled floors. This is a young, enthusiastic, family-run place to stay. *Self-contained cottage available. Central heating. BBQs for groups in summer. Historic towns nearby; 100 metres to arts and crafts. Platypuses can be seen in their natural habitat just 500m away.*

Rooms: 6: 1 king and 5 queens, all with en/s showers. 1 cottage is self-contained incl spa, gas-fire, 1 queen and 1 single (min 2-night stay in cottage).
Price: $135 – $240. Singles $99 – $110, but not on Saturday nights.
Meals: Full gourmet breakfast included, light suppers by prior arrangement.
Directions: From Sydney, take M5 towards Canberra for 123km. 2nd sign to Berrima follow into village and through town. Last road to the left is Oxley St. House on right.
Postal Address: PO Box 1973, Berrima 2577.

Chelsea Park

Davidia Williams
589 Moss Vale Rd, Burradoo 2576
Tel: 02-4861-7046 Fax: 02-4862-3597
Email: chelsea@hinet.net.au Web: www.chelseapark.com

Davidia is locked in an adoring embrace with all things art deco. Her 1946 home pays homage to the movement at every turn, with its pastel-coloured walls and carpets and grand curved staircase with wrought-iron banister. All the furniture, paintings, prints of transatlantic liners, the collection of toy buses and cars, even the tea sets and china have been hunted down and bought from dealers, auctions and the internet. It's an art deco world all right. For the B&B Davidia has installed the best of everything: carpets are the sort you want to pad about on; bedrooms are large and warm, towels white and engulfing; there are bathrobes for walking to the two next door (not en-suite) bathrooms, one with a spa bath (first come, first served), one with a walk-in shower; and there are electric blankets for winter (these are the highlands and nights can get nippy). Everything is sturdy and well-made. There is a billiard room, by the way, and upstairs a second sitting-room for guests seeking more privacy. Davidia has so much room at Chelsea Park that she could easily have created more bedrooms. But guests are the ones who benefit from so much space and attention. *Bowral is home to the Bradman Museum and "Bade" Country National Parks and is famous for books and antiques.*

Rooms: 2: 1 queen and 1 queen/twin with 1 spa bath/shower and 1 shower.
Price: $145 – $190. $300 for 2 nights at the weekend. Singles $140.
Meals: Full breakfast included. Complimentary supper on one night if staying 2 nights or more – crusty bread, soup, pasta, quiche etc.
Directions: From Sydney take freeway towards Canberra. Turn off Mittagong thro' Bowral, follow signs to Moss Vale – house signed on R.

Map Number: 3 &

The Harp B&B

Marlene Bell

Illawarra Highway, Sutton Forest 2577
Tel: 02-4869-2650 Fax: 02-4869-2650
Email: Web: www.highlandsnsw.com.au/theharp
Cell: 0412-659-528

The ghosts of landlords long gone must be delighted with the way Marlene has re-established this B&B. The Harp was built as an inn in the 1830s before falling into disrepair in recent years, but now the tradition of hospitality and merriment is once more thriving in Sutton Forest. This is a place to get up late and potter around. There are two sitting-rooms – one with a TV, one with a fire (oh the decisions!) – but you'll probably end up in the 'gallery'. This light-filled room acts as a sort of internal verandah, connecting the house to the 1820s kitchen (21st-century standards, of course). The gallery is the hub, offering music, more sofas and Marlene's big breakfasts. She fizzes around all of this, full of projects for the garden – five acres leading down to the creek – and the Coach House, but ever ready with a mug of coffee and a dash of Aussie humour to keep you ticking along. The restoration has been as successful in the bedrooms as elsewhere; there are two downstairs (ask for the main one) with big beds, timber walls and antique wardrobes, and the large, pale, wooden loft suite has space to swing several cats, although these are not supplied. *Sutton Forest is about 1.5 hours from Sydney and Canberra, and surrounding towns are full of antique and book shops.*

Rooms: 3: 1 king/twin en-suite shower; 1 king/twin en-suite shower/bath; 1 loft suite with 1 dbl room and 2 singles in lounge, bathroom with shower.
Price: $390 – $410 for TWO nights at weekends. $140 – $150 per night during the week. Single rates on request.
Meals: Full breakfast included.
Directions: From Sydney turn L to Sutton Forest off the M5 (turn-off after Berrima). Come into village and turn R at T-jct (onto Illawarra Highway). House is 600m on the R. Map available on web site.

Markdale Homestead

Geoff and Mary Ashton
Markdale, Binda 2583
Tel: 02-4835-3146 or 02-9327-2191 Fax: 02-4835-3160
Email: gashton@compuserve.com Web: www.markdale.com

Those who travel through the countryside of the Southern Tablelands to Markdale encounter something quite special: a house, a garden and a family woven into Australia's past in a mesmerisingly peaceful setting. This 8,000-acre sheep and cattle farm is Geoff's ancestral homestead. His father and three uncles achieved fame as the polo-playing Ashton brothers who represented Australia in the 1930s and frequently beat the Brits. So no change there. Markdale is grand, from the homestead (built in the 1920s), to the rural setting, to the Edna Walling-designed garden. Guests stay in two 19th-century cottages on the property a few minutes from the homestead. You'll probably end up wandering repeatedly backwards and forwards. The five-acre garden is an asymmetrical delight with small lawns, flowing lines and nooks aplenty. There's a dam with rowing boat and island, wisteria-clad archways coaxing you to the tennis court and a polo practice pit dating from the 1930s. I confirmed what I already knew by falling off the 'horse'. The cottages are lived-in, comfortable and full of polo memorabilia. There are big fires, lots of flowers and verandahs with views across Ashton-shire. It's a great farm for watching seasonal activities or for exploring, with an old slab hut, shearing sheds, ten kilometres of trout-fishing and long walks.

Rooms: Stone House: 2 dbl, 1 tw, 1 bunk; 1 en-suite shower, 1 separate bath. Annexe: 1 dbl, 1 tw, 1 shower. Both cottages have kitchens and sitting-rooms.
Price: Stone House: $75 – $100 p.p. Exclusive use $500 for up to 8 people. Annexe: $100 p.p. Exclusive use $250 up to 4 people. Less if staying 2 nights or more.
Meals: Self-cook breakfast provisions provided. Self-cater for dinner, or pre-cooked meals available.
Directions: 80km NW of Goulburn. From Goulburn go NW to Crookwell then 20km to Binda. 9km beyond Binda turn L towards Bigga. After 5km turn L to Markdale. 3.5km of sealed road then 2km of gravel rd to hse. Directions can be faxed.

Map Number: 4 & 5

Jaspers Brush B&B and Alpaca Farm

Léonie and Ian Winlaw
465 Strongs Rd, Jaspers Brush 2535
Tel: 02-4448-6194 Fax: 02-4448-6254
Email: iwinlaw@ozemail.com.au Web: www.jaspersbrushbandb.com.au
Cell: 0418-116655

Jaspers Brush stands high on the Berry escarpment with remarkable views across its own lush garden and alpaca paddocks (yes, the Andean camelid with the fleece), over forests and all the way to Jervis Bay and Gerringong. It truly is a heavenly sight... and heaven for birds too (binoculars and guide book provided). There are alpaca-fleece (of course) doonas on richly dressed beds, and enormous showers, while two of the bedrooms have doors that open onto a wrap-around verandah with chairs positioned just so for that view. Guests share a sitting-room where breakfast is served. This is not only delicious (fresh orange juice, fresh fruit platter, a perfectly poached egg from the Winlaws' own hens), but presented with great care too. Léonie and Ian are charming and amusing hosts who travel widely and are keen art collectors (I admired their walls and knowledge equally). Former Sydney-dwellers, they love their lives on the south coast as much as the alpacas, which potter surreally in the background. Guests arriving before dusk can probably join Ian for feeding time, but everyone should walk to the top of the property, from where the panorama is supreme. *A range of alpaca products available. Walking, bird-watching, beaches, dolphins, whales, golf, horses, Kangaroo Valley all nearby.*

Rooms: 3: 2 doubles, 1 with en/s bathroom and 1 with private bathroom; 1 twin with en/s bathroom. All with showers only.
Price: $176 (twin room) – $220 (verandah rooms) per night w/ends or holidays (min 2 nights). Weekday rates $154 (twin) – $198 (verandah rooms). Includes GST.
Meals: Full breakfast is included.
Directions: From Sydney, take Princes Highway to Berry. Go 5km beyond Berry, turn right into Strongs Road. Continue for 4.65km passing through Burnside Gate until you reach sign to Jaspers Brush on left.
Postal Address: PO Box 308, Berry 2535.

Map Number: 5

Paperbark Camp

Jeremy and Irena Hutchings
571 Woollamia Rd, Huskisson, Jervis Bay 2540
Tel: 02-4441-6066 Fax: 02-4441-6066
Email: info@paperbarkcamp.com.au Web: www.paperbarkcamp.com.au

Just two and a half hours from Sydney, here is a wonderful place to escape for a honeymoon wedding anniversary, birthday… or weekend of whimsy. Some of Australia's best beaches are within easy reach and you sleep in highly original (in Australia) African safari tents deep in the bush. Paperbark Camp is an eco-lodge and a genuine attempt to protect this very Australian silva environment: everything is done for the good of the forest. The food (served at the Gunyah, a large building raised to tree level) really is excellent, but also there is an exciting feeling of being somewhere unusual and special. As for those tents... they are spaced out in the woods, raised high above ground on stilts, with a deck at the front and a semi-outdoor shower, loo and basin at the back. This is camping, but in great comfort. The dawn chorus, conducted by the male kookaburras, is an unforgettable way to meet the day. There's canoeing on the creek (just launch and go); walking trails in the bush; bird-, dolphin- and whale-watching; diving and swimming off the whitest sand beaches known to man… or idling down at the pub in Huskisson gazing out to sea. *Paperbark should be licensed by the time of publication of this second edition. Ask about kids.*

Rooms: 10 safari-style tents out in the bush (but not too far!). 6 queens and 4 kings/twins, all with en-suite shower. 4 tents have extra dbl futon.
Price: $360 per couple per night including dinner, bed and breakfast, min 2 nights. Singles $225 per night, min 2 nights. Enquire about single-night prices.
Meals: Full breakfast and 3-course à la carte dinner included.
Directions: From Sydney take Princes Highway south, 13km past Nowra turn L to Jervis Bay/Huskisson. After 2km L signed Woollamia. "PC" 6km in trees on L, just after Goodland Rd.
Closed: July and August.
Postal Address: PO Box 39, Huskisson 2540.

Map Number:

Nelligen Gallery – B&B

Kay Faulkner and Brian Reader
13 Braidwood St, Nelligen 2536
Tel: 02-4478-1163
Email: kay@nelligen.com Web: www.nelligen.com

I find that great places to stay often offer new, self-contained universes, extensions of the people that live there. The Gallery is just such a place. You are given the entire cottage, a labyrinth of staircases, decks and unexpected alcoves which reflect the character and charm of this 1860s building. After hours, you have the actual gallery to yourselves too. The cottage is awash with flowers, a traveller's collection of artefacts – large puppets, Burmese umbrellas as lampshades – and intriguing pieces by emerging artists. The cosy, atticky bedroom has a huge bed piled with white pillows, a fireplace and a giant pane of glass that allows magnificent views down over the Clyde River. The river is the focus of the house, stretching away between dense eucalypt forests with no development for 108 kilometres upstream. You can sit mesmerised on the verandah alongside the local wildlife or admire it all from the comfort of fireside or bed. You are surrounded by national parks, there are magnificent beaches close by and Canberra is just an hour and a half away. Book as far in advance as you can as Kay and Brian can take only one couple here, although they also have a self-catering cottage 5km away on the farm, overlooking a tidal pool.

Rooms: 1 queen-size with private bathroom, sitting-room with open fire, dining-room and kitchen, numerous decks.
Price: From $160.
Meals: Full breakfast or hamper included at a time of your choosing. There are excellent restaurants in Batemans Bay. Cafés and bistro in Nelligen.
Directions: Turn R as you enter Batemans Bay (from Sydney) signed Braidwood/Canberra. 8km to Nelligen, over the river and turn L into village and then R, then R again up steeper side of Braidwood St. Gallery B&B (in the Old Watch-house) is second on the R.

The Priory at Bingie

Barbara and Nick Romalis
Priory Lane, Bingie, via Moruya 2537
Tel: 02-4473-8881 Fax: 02-4473-8881
Email: thepriory@bingie.com Web: www.bingie.com

The Priory will open the sensory pores and rejuvenate any latent artistic inclinations you ma
have. Barbara fashions delicate leaves from copper, complicated metal cockatoos and oversize
insects. But there are paintings, pottery and printed fabrics everywhere, her own and that
colleagues (much is for sale). Nick and Barbara built this stylish Greek-style house to their ow
specifications on fifty acres of open hilltop, surrounded by gardens and sloping paddocks full
kangaroos. The property looks straight out to sea and you can stroll down to the dunes and beac
from the house – an Aboriginal guide will take you to the point. Breakfast or dinner in fine weathe
is on the roof terrace and judging by the oven-baked bread that spread desire throughout th
house while I was there, I can only assume that the food will heap excellence on excellence. A
first glance you can tell that nothing will be merely ordinary. The tour of the house saw smok
rise from the nib of my pen: marble bathrooms with sea views, a sit-down shower, an 1864 gran
piano, a barrel-vaulted ceiling, oceans of marble floor studded with fossils and laid out with rich
coloured rugs from all over the world. No more space here. Go and see for yourself. *No mobi
phone conversations in public areas!*

Rooms: 3: all doubles; 1 with en-suite bath and
shower; 2 with en-suite shower over bath. 1 is self-
contained with kitchen.
Price: $170. Singles $75.
Meals: Full breakfast included and served till 10.
Dinner by prior arrangement: $45 – $50 for 4
courses (BYO wine).
Directions: From Sydney take Princes Highway
south for 4.5 hours. 9km past Moruya turn L signed
Bingie Rd. Follow straight for 1km to T Jct. Turn R,
down and straight up hill to house.

Green Gables B&B

Stuart Absalom and Philip Mawer

269 Corkhill Drive, Tilba Tilba 2546
Tel: 02-4473-7435
Email:
relax@greengables.com.au
Web:
www.greengables.com.au

I confess that I haven't actually been to Green Gables, as Stuart and Philip made their move too late for us to visit. But I have no problem recommending it, as we already know what great hosts they are and count them as GG stalwarts! Until recently they ran a very popular B&B called Heathville in Melbourne that we featured in the first edition of this guide. For a change of scene and a taste of the countryside, they have upped sticks and resettled in this delightful, almost Tolkienesque New South Wales landscape. The Tilbas (I *do* know the Tilbas) are adorable twins, tiny heritage (late nineteenth-century) villages hidden amid a swell of undulating hills and surrounded by green pastureland. Green Gables itself was built in 1879 and sits beneath Mt Dromedary (or sacred Gulaga). Breakfast, often taken on one of the wide verandahs, can take all morning if you want to linger, as guests often make friends with each other in such a friendly environment. There is loads to do in the region, including fishing and bush-walking, with beaches and national parks nearby and many cottage industries like cheese- and wine-making on your doorstep. As long as your hosts are at the helm you will have found the most homely, relaxed place to base yourself in the area.

Rooms: 3: 2 queens with en-suite shower and 1 queen/twin with private bathroom.
Price: $130 – $140. Singles $90 – $100.
Meals: Full breakfast included. Dinner by arrangement: $30 – $40.
Directions: Will be faxed or emailed.

Bimbimbi House

Peter and Beverley Bray

62 Nutleys Creek Rd,
Bermagui 2546
Tel: 02-6493-4456
Fax: 02-6493-4456
Email:
bimbimbihouse@bigfoot.com.au

From the first-floor verandah you gaze over a thick carpet of orange Brazilian creeper, across eight acres of mature garden, down the hill framed by the branches of widely-spaced gum trees to the Bermagui River and Jaggers Bay below. Bimbimbi has about an acre of river frontage at the bottom of the property. It's pretty perfect actually. Beverley and Peter have taken the big step of leaving the rat race in Melbourne for a seaside life in this quirky, rambling, charming 1940s farmhouse. Now they chew the fat with their guests, eat fresh oysters, fish for flathead and king dory from Bermagui Harbour, tend a sheep and a cow, bring the great old garden back into line, restore the dry stone walls, feed the rosellas and parrots. All this is at your disposal as guests of course. You either take the apartment complete with enormous bedroom, sitting-room, kitchen, pantry and direct access to the verandah – surely one of the most enticing breakfasting spots in the country – or the garden room downstairs which is the Brays' own favourite. You can self-cater, but a full, never-boring breakfast is provided every day with quiche, yoghurt, home-made bread, local cheeses etc. I imagine taking the place for a week and digging in. (That's what Billy Connolly did!) *2km to beach. Enquire about kids. Self-catering cottage also available.*

Rooms: 3: 1 suite with 2 bedrooms, bath, shower; 1 room with en-suite shower; 1 self-catering cottage.
Price: $130 – $170. Singles $100.
Meals: Full breakfast included. Cook your own dinners in kitchen provided.
Directions: From Sydney take Princes Highway south for 5.5 hours approx. Take first L signed Bermagui. Into town, over bridge, 1st R into Bridge St, round bend 1st R into Nutleys Creek Rd. House is up on R.

Map Number: 4 & 5

Rock Lily Cottages

Delphine Troughear

864 Warrigal Range Rd, Brogo, via Bega 2550
Tel: 02-6492-7364 Fax: 02-6492-7363
Email: info@rocklily.com.au Web: www.rocklily.com.au

With wide, high views of the Wadbilliga National Park and Wilderness, Delphine's charming mud-brick and timber cottages sit in proud isolation. The beams come from old bridges and railway sleepers, the washbasins are antique, windows are old restored lead lights, beds are mainly brass (although I enjoyed a mahogany four-poster in Woodruff) and all in all they have a warm, wooden, well-made feeling that encourages you to spend time indoors as well as out. In case of bad weather the cottages are well stocked with TV, video or DVD, stereo, library and games – and fresh flowers are laid out for your arrival. Two even have record-players with selections of LPs to spin upon them. The starter breakfast hamper contains a generous supply of bacon, free-range eggs, freshly home-made bread, jars of jam, ground coffee, a selection of teas, berry and nut muesli, milk and juice. Delphine reckons the hamper lasts between one and two days for most guests. The two mud-brick cottages are set on 100 acres of native bushland with old Port Jackson figs and rock lilies growing out of granite boulders, while Woodruff occupies its own 16 acres and is idyllically positioned high on a hill with valley and mountain views and wombats below the verandah. *Some air-conditioning. All are dog-friendly. Brogo Dam is just down the road for canoeing, swimming and bass fishing.*

Rooms: 3 cottages: 2 with 1 bedroom, queen-size with en/s shower; 1 with 2 bedrooms, 1 queen en/s shower, 1 family sharing shower.
Price: From $150 ($35 an extra bed). Singles from $140.
Meals: Self-catering, but a large starter breakfast hamper is provided.
Directions: 18km north of Bega (20km south of Cobargo) take the turn-off to the Brogo Dam. Drive 8.5km towards the dam. Rock Lily is on the right-hand side and well sign-posted.

Map Number: 4 & 5

Bumblebrook Farm Motel

Rick and Ann Patten
Kemps Lane, Candelo 2550
Tel: 02-6493-2238 Fax: 02-6493-2299
Email: bumblebrook@acr.net.au Web: www.bumblebrook.com.au

Really friendly hosts, beautiful hilly setting and fantastic good value – I'm proud of this one. Th
land was given as a reward to a soldier returning from the First World War and is now th
property of a sailor – Rick was in the Australian navy in a former life. Guests stay in motel-styl
units housed in a bungalow a hundred metres from the main house, the path between the tw
lit by hurricane lamps. The units are combinations of brick and wood, all with verandahs. Dor
expect luxury here – you're not paying for it – but you will be comfortable and have all that yo
need: kitchens, sofas, separate sitting-rooms in the two family-units and somewhere beautiful t
sit. The views are a heady combination of sloping fields, eucalyptus trees and the distant hills o
Indian Head. It's a ten-minute walk down to swimming holes in the river and the Pattens ca
show you walks. Rates include a breakfast basket of farm eggs, bacon, home-made jam, home
made bread, juice and cereals, and in the evening, you can self-cater (oven or BBQ) or indulg
yourself up at the house where Ann does suppers. Finally, this is an excellent spot for childre
with a tree-house, small play area, lots of farm animals to feed – cows, goats, donkeys, chicken
dogs and cat.

Rooms: 4 units, all have shower-rooms, all have
double beds and 2 have sitting-rooms.
Price: $90 – $115. Singles $75 – $100. Extra perso
$15 – $20. Weekly rates minus 10%. Children unde
13 free.
Meals: Full cook-your-own breakfast basket
provided. Dinner by arrangement: 3 courses with
drinks $40 p.p., $25 for kids.
Directions: From Bega follow signs to Eden, then
turn off in Candelo. In Candelo cross main bridge on
your right, then turn R towards Bemboka/Cooma. It
is 4km to Kemps Lane and Bumblebrook is just down
here on the left.
Postal Address: PO Box 26, Candelo 2550.

Map Number: 4 &

The Outpost

Jill and David Madew

Yaouk Valley, Adaminaby 2630
Tel: 02-6454-2293
Fax: 02-6454-2293
Email: jill@theoutpost.com.au
Web: www.theoutpost.com.au

This rare and remarkable place leads you miles from the world of man, then rewards you with an enchanting oasis of civilisation. Jill bought the property – no road, no house, no nothing – in 1985 and established a fishing lodge. Now in 'retirement', she and David offer a self-catering cottage (rented to one group at a time) near the main house, with two simple bedrooms, a large kitchen and a wood-burning stove to counteract the night chill (the cottage is at 1100 metres). You can picnic down by the river, up in the hills or on the large rock at the end of the garden, which juts out above the water and provides the most perfect of views. The Outpost sits in 1000 acres of mostly untouched eucalyptus forest and the cottage is barely 70 metres from the Murrumbidgee River. There are great walks, deep swimming holes (watch for platypuses), a tennis court, a 'bush' croquet lawn and, of course, excellent fly-fishing (obtain a licence in advance). I arrived at dusk, one eye carefully watching for jay-bounding kangaroos and the other cherishing the views along the 29 km of dirt roads – including 4 km of driveway – that lead here from Adaminaby. Where you can buy food, by the way. Jill supplies full breakfast provisions and provides suppers with a bit of prior notice. Give yourself at *least* two nights. *Canberra 2.5 hours away.*

Rooms: 1 cottage with 2 bedrooms (queen and twin), shower room and extra loo.
Price: $180 per night for 1 or 2 people if staying 2 nights. Less for longer stays. Extra people $15 p.p.p.n. 2% charged for credit card payments.
Meals: Self-cook breakfast $10 per person: bacon, eggs, cereal, home-made marmalade etc. 3-course dinner can be delivered to cottage for $75 p.p. including wine.
Directions: Will be given on booking. 29km from Adaminaby.

Avalanche Homestead

Frank and Faye Biddle

1126 Urila Rd, Burra Creek 2620
Tel: 02-6236-3245 Fax: 02-6236-3302
Email: info@avalanchehomestead.com
Web: www.avalanchehomestead.com

I'd been concentrating so hard on keeping my car on the dirt road – the rain had made it slipper – that I hadn't noticed the burgeoning scenery. I got the picture when I unfolded myself from th seat and beheld (no other word for it) mountains that seemed to have suddenly stood up from nowhere, low cloud lying between peaks like snow… and nearer to the lodge, kangaroo hopping about in the paddocks. I was swept up and in by Frank and Faye, introduced to everyone given a glass of beer and we didn't stop chatting until an exquisite dinner came to an end hour later. Amazingly, neither of our hosts ever seemed to be absent and yet there was definitely no one else helping in the kitchen… spooky! Finally Frank got us into rain gear and took us for a nigh drive on the farm to see the kangaroos and wombats – quite beautiful, the gum leaves twinklin like Christmas lights in the rain. The bedrooms at the main house line up Aussie homestead style quaintly out-of-date with sliding doors out to the pool area. Avalanche has great character and the food is truly delicious. *Masses to do, including horse-riding, 4x4 tours, lake fishing, bird-watching (5 species), shearing (doing, not just watching), rounding up cattle; they also run tours from Sydney t Melbourne via Avalanche.*

Rooms: 7: 6 double/twins with en-suite shower; 1 double/twin with en-suite spa bath (shower above).
Price: $230 per person per night. Includes all meals, wine with dinner and activities on the property (see above).
Meals: Full breakfast, lunch and 3-course dinner included.
Directions: From Sydney to Canberra, then to Queanbeyan. From Main St in Q turn into Lowe St, F at roundabout into Cooma St, 12km L into Burra Rd, 12km L into Urila Rd, straight for 12km dirt road to house.
Postal Address: PO Box 544, Queanbeyan 2620.

Map Number: 4 & 5

Woodstock

Sarah and Michael Retallack

Uriarra 2611
Tel: 02-6236-5151 Fax: 02-6236-5129
Email: woodstoc@webone.com.au
Cell: 0413-617-547

Bush fires almost consigned the Woodstock homestead to its doom in 2003. The flames got to within 30 metres of Sarah and Michael's beloved old house before the buildings were saved. A huge relief not only for the family – daughter Clementine is now the fifth generation of Retallacks at Woodstock – but also for all those of us who enjoy staying at family-run farms with friendly hosts and beautiful environments. Guests are treated with rare style on this 4,000-acre sheep and cattle farm, with flowers in the bedrooms and silver on the table. Drought and fire have temporarily altered the landscape, but this will always be a superb property, bounded by the Brindabella Mountains and the Murrumbidgee River, with two more creeks and a 30-foot waterfall to boot. Sarah ran a catering company in London before marrying her Australian beau and she knows a bit about the hostly arts. I couldn't stay for dinner, but 'spicy roast pumpkin', 'Thai salmon filo parcels', 'grilled winter fruit and fig ice cream'?... this is not simple farm fare. Guests have their own elegant dining-room, a drawing-room full of photos, paintings and antiques, and two bedrooms. The Retallacks want visitors to "get on with their own thing", so I suggest you do. Walk around the property, swim in the pool, laze in the garden, visit Canberra. Despite the farm's isolation, Parliament House is just 25 minutes away.

Rooms: 2: 1 queen with en-suite bath (shower above); 1 double with private shower.
Price: $130 – $180. No single rate. Children's rates negotiable.
Meals: Full breakfast included. Dinner $40 – $50 p.p. for 3 courses. BYO.
Directions: From Canberra, leave Parliament House on Adelaide Ave. Take 4th L onto Cotter Rd. Turn R (signed Belconnen/Uriarra) and go 13km crossing Murrumbidgee. Then bear R & Woodstock is 2km on R. Or directions faxed.

Yabtree

Noela and Fred Horsley
Tumblong 2729
Tel: 02-6944-7571 Fax: 02-6944-7552
Email: yabtree@bigpond.com Web: www.yabtree.com.au

Here is one of the best reasons for you to have bought this book. A few hundred miles and ten cattle grids will eventually see you drawing up an avenue of English elms (a rare sight if you happen to be English) to an oasis of tall palm trees. I arrived at the hottest hour on the hottest day for ten years (46 degrees on the verandah!) and we literally had to dive into the air-conditioning (this is not typical I should point out). Fred represents the fourth generation of Horsleys to live in the 1840s homestead. It is a wonderful house of marble, mirror and wood with a 'breeze-way' of ornamental grape and wisteria, a full-size billiard room, a family graveyard, an original settler's hut, pressed metal ceilings, old sash windows, a collection of modern art, a National Trust garden... and, outside, a delicious-looking swimming pool. You are welcomed as proper house guests, everyone dining together. If you are very lucky, Noela will organise a silver service dinner down on the banks of the Murrumbidgee, which flows through the property. By day you can lounge by the pool, walk in the garden or down by the river, visit the cattle and sheep farm with Fred, take books from shelves, play music, tennis or snooker. If it helps, Barbara Streisand loved her time at Yabtree. Another one of those places where I can almost hear you thanking me already!

Rooms: 3: 1 unit with 2 doubles and 2 singles sharing a shower and bath; 2 doubles in house sharing shower; 1 extra bath. (Can accommodate up to 10 friends.)
Price: $165 per person including dinner.
Meals: Full breakfast and dinner included (pre-dinner nibbles, 2 courses with drinks).
Directions: From the Hume Highway going north 15km north of Tarcutta – go left into Deltroit Rd. Follow dirt road and signs to Yabtree for 10km.
Closed: Christmas – New Year.

Map Number: 4 & 5

Victoria

Anchorage

Tricia and Chris Wain
11 The Anchorage, Metung 3904
Tel: 03-5156-2569 Fax: 03-5156-2569
Email: anchoragebandb@bigpond.com
Web: www.anchoragebedandbreakfast.com.au Cell: 0407-762-569

In a way this is my favourite sort of place. From the outside, a suburban court in the shape of keyhole (à la *Neighbours*), a door in a bungalow, a ding-dong bell… Many would drive away wi low expectations and Trish says many do! But they are making a big mistake. Wains' world is revelation. Trish is greatly humorous with the happy knack of putting you instantly at ease. Th main living area of the house is open-plan with stone-tiled floor, rattan blinds, wicker and woo furniture, family photos on the walls, jolly colours. Add to this sunny scene some jazz, the waft real coffee and some lovely, unanticipated views and my misgivings evaporated before I ha crossed the threshhold. Trish finally got her cup of coffee in the bright breakfast area, which lea out onto wooden decks with views down to Chinaman's Creek and the boats and jetties. Th creek runs into Bancroft Bay, a large lake, and on the other side is a narrow strip of land th separates off the sea and Ninety Mile Beach. The two bedrooms are downstairs with their ow access, bright, new and modern with colourful duvets, fridge and telly, tea and coffee, bathrobe heater, fan, lots of green towels. This is the sort of B&B where the warmth of place and perso combine to lift the spirits. *Charter boats on the lakes; free-range kangaroos and koalas on Raymor Island.*

Rooms: 2: both queens with en/s showers.
Price: $130 – $150. Singles $110 – $120.
Meals: Full breakfast included.
Directions: From Princess Highway turn towards Metung into the village. Signed right up hill at Chinaman's Creek – keep right where the road fork continue to Anchorage (house at bottom of court).
Postal Address: PO Box 164, Metung 3904.

Map Number:

Vereker House

Mary and John O'Shea

10 Iluka Close, Foley Rd, Yanakie, South Gippsland 3960
Tel: 03-5687-1431 Fax: 03-5687-1480
Email: vereker@tpg.com.au Web: www.vereker.com

It's not every day that you get to meet a *bona fide* Antarctic explorer. John spent 14 months on the icy desert with the Bureau of Meteorology in the 1970s and this erudite Irish émigré's tales from that time are fascinating. It's a world far removed from Wilsons Prom, whose verdant prominence looms in the background as we chat beside a crackling open fire. John built Vereker House to withstand the variable environment, utilising an atypical post-and-beam structure and adobe bricks. The result is a solid building full of rustic timber; you'll see Cyprus pine, Douglas fir and red cedar used throughout, from the cathedral ceiling of the lounge to the wood-panelling in the bedrooms. What makes Vereker House so special is John and Mary's extensive knowledge of the fauna and flora of Australia's southernmost lobe. In the evenings, over wholesome Australian fare and a drop of the local grape or grain, there's the opportunity to pick their brains. Breakfast is served in a bright conservatory, where, beyond a flurry of native birds imbibing their morning nectar, you can fortify yourself with a maritime panorama of the Yanakie Valley climbing the foothills of Mount Vereker. Although exactly for whom the mountain, and consequently the house, is named is subject to debate, one look in its direction and John will give you the forecast for the day. An excellent base-camp from which to conduct your own explorations.

Rooms: 4: 3 queens and 1 twin, all with en-suite shower.
Price: $130 – $150. Singles from $110.
Meals: Full breakfast included. Dinner by arrangement $44 per person.
Directions: Follow signs to Wilsons Promontory, through Yanakie. Foley Road is on left-hand side. Vereker House appears on your right.
Postal Address: PO Box 61, Foster 3960.

Larkrise House

Jon and Ros Wathen
395 Fish Creek – Foster Rd, Foster 3960
Tel: 03-5682-2953 Fax: 03-5682-2951
Email: jonandros@larkrise.com.au Web: www.larkrise.com.au

Jon and Ros stayed here themselves once and, like Victor Kiam, liked it so much they bought the place! Theirs is a friendliness that greets you on arrival and chats easily over home-made apple cake. There are clues to Jon and Ros's lineage throughout their comfortable home. Beside the four-poster bed are lithographs of Tasmania, a gift from the bank, and Jon's grandmother's delicate floral illustrations. Much of the antique furniture originates from Norfolk, the GG heartland. Points awarded for that. I became quite misty-eyed when Jon pointed out the old mahogany table expatriated from my local Aylsham pub. There we were, an East Anglian triumvirate, perfectly home in this Australian setting. The undeniable pull here is the sprawling coastal vista, which the house takes full advantage of. A sitting-room morphs into a slate-floored conservatory, showcasing the expansive sweep of Wilsons Promontory. The bedrooms share the views, looking across paddocks policed by two old Shetlands. Snaking its way through virgin blackwood forest the edge of their property is the scenic Rail Trail. There's a terrace at the back of the house shaded by a tenacious vine, and beyond the hedging camellias you'll find a rare site: a spa that been taken out and turned into a fernery… points for that, too!

Rooms: 2: both queens with en-suite showers. Possibly adding two new rooms in winter 2004.
Price: $130 – $160. Singles $110 – $140.
Meals: Full breakfast included. Evening meals on weekend or by request. 3 courses and coffee $40.
Directions: From Foster follow signs to Fish Creek, 3km along Fish Creek Rd. From Wilsons Promontory 2nd left to Fish Creek from Foster Rd.

Dreamers Mountain Village

Mal and Wendy Lee

Kiewa Valley Highway, Tawonga South 3699
Tel: 03-5754-1222 Fax: 03-5754-1333
Email: dreamers@albury.net.au Web: www.dreamers1.com

It's a perk of this job that you encounter magnificent places, people and scenery. In this last, little can rival the Great Alpine Road. The views from Mt Hotham are amongst the best in Victoria. Or so I'm told. It was pitch dark when I reached the summit and edged my car through enveloping cloud. After such a harrowing trip, Dreamers Mountain came as welcome refuge. I was met by a cheery Wendy, who pointed me to the local takeaway. Fresh lasagne in hand, I drove out to my own ash-panelled cocoon, lit a fire in the sunken den and soaked in the spa. In the morning, Mal served me breakfast on a deck cantilevered over a trout-filled lagoon. The day was ablaze with the fiery colour of autumn's first burst and hummed to the sound of a docile tractor and the chatter of inquisitive geese. Mal and Wendy have created an idyll in the foothills of Mt Bogong. Inspired by Queensland's vast wool-stores, the four steel-framed, corrugated-iron-roofed chalets are individually themed with a strong emphasis on renewable energy… and romance. Beyond the stone swimming pool, there's a cavernous, barn-doored guesthouse showcasing Mal's handiwork. After a dinner at the hand-made liquid amber and marble banqueting table, warm yourself by the open fire, then slip into the glass bath in your French-styled bedroom. Sometimes magnificent places, people and scenery all converge at the same spot. Come and see for yourself.

Rooms: 5: 4 chalets with queen plus loft-style double, spa bath and shower. Barnhouse has 1 queen sharing a private sh and 1 king/twin with glass bath.

Price: $160 – $230. Singles $110.

Meals: Full breakfast extra $30 – $40 for 2. Meal platters from local restaurant by arrangement: about $48 p.p.

Directions: From Melbourne turn off Hume Fwy at BP & McDonald's just Sth of Wangaratta towards Myrtleford. From Myrtleford go east (at Ovens) to Kiewa Valley Hwy, then Sth to Mt Beauty. "DMV" on L on edge of Mt Beauty.

Postal Address: PO Box 310, Mt Beauty 3699.

Map Number: 4 & 5

The Bank Restaurant and Mews

Wayne McLaughlin

86 Ford St, Beechworth 3747
Tel: 03-5728-2223
Fax: 03-5728-2883
Email:
info@thebankrestaurant.com
Web:
www.thebankrestaurant.com

The Bank is the special place in town for two reasons: for the restaurant itself and for Wayne whose enthusiasm and natural, genuine way with people creates its own atmosphere. He admi that nothing gives him so much pleasure as seeing his guests sitting round the outside table chatting away under green parasols, perhaps during Sunday lunch on a warm day. This is in fact formal restaurant and the food is extremely good. I know because I have eaten there. And th building, built in 1856, was once a Bank of Australasia. The original Victorian gadgetry remain intact: wooden security screens hidden in the window sills are ready to spring up to the 18-foo ceilings (no less!) and protect their windows; and the old gold vault makes a perfect wine cella and many diners poke their heads in for a look. The whole compound is walled in an overnighters sleep in the converted stables at the back. Here you have lots of space and light, b iron beds and all you could need in the way of telly, CD player, bathroom bits and bobs, mini ba etc. The great thing is to eat at the restaurant and to be a part of The Bank experience for at lea one night. In the words of one of The Bank's regulars: 'It's an oasis of civilisation.' *Historic tow tours.*

Rooms: 4: all queen-size with en/s shower.
Price: $160 – $170.
Meals: Rate includes Continental "Butler's breakfast" (poached fruit and muesli) brought to room. Restaurant has an à la carte menu every night.
Directions: Right in the centre of Beechworth by the Post Office.

Map Number: 4 &

Sunnymeade B&B

Margaret, John and Craig Irving

RMB 4610, Boundary Hill Rd,
Strathbogie via Euroa 3666
Tel: 03-5790-8519
Fax: 03-5790-8518
Email:
sunnymeade@bigpond.com
Web:
www.sunnymeade.com.au

I was told that in the middle of Victoria there existed a formal English garden of extraordinary proportions. It didn't begin to prepare me for what really is one of the most fantastical sights I've seen on my travels around Australia. I arrived out of the blue, around noon (a classic trick), and Margaret and Craig very sweetly shared their lunch with me. Then we toured the interconnecting garden rooms, Margaret papering over the cracks in my horticultural knowledge by calling out the botanical names as we passed a dazzling array of hedges, perennials and climbers. There's a laburnum tunnel, box parterre and espaliered pears; a gazebo, a tower, even a Persian pavilion. Sunnymeade is a labour of love, a folly of whimsy and a testament to one man's extraordinary talent. A self-taught botanist, viticulturist and stone-mason, Craig planted all this himself, finding inspiration in English gardens such as Hidcote (the pleached hornbeam hedges) and gardeners like Gertrude Jekyll (the crescendo of colour in the summer border). The award-winning garden is open to visitors, but you really should stay. It's no surprise that Craig built the walled-in cottage overlooking the cool-climate vineyard. With pine dado boards and hand-stenciled walls, this sandstone sanctuary is stocked with Sunnymeade wine and home-made jams, which you can share with the rosellas and wrens on the verandah. I really can't recommend it enough.

Rooms: 1 self-catering cottage with shower.
Price: $150 – $185. $30 an extra bed.
Meals: Breakfast provided in the fridge.
Directions: Coming from Melbourne, leave the Hume Freeway at Euroa. Take Strathbogie Road from Euroa and go 17km to junction. Turn left into Creek Junction Road and follow Sunnymeade signs to the property in Boundary Hill Road.

Map Number: 5

Camerons by the Falls

Andrew and Elly Cameron

The Falls, RMB 2750, Euroa 3666
Tel: 03-5798-5291 Fax: 03-5798-5437
Email: thefalls@euroa.net.au Web: www.cameronsbythefalls.com.au

From the warm welcome to the final adieu, Camerons embodies all that we look for in a place to stay. It is a home so comfortable that it is almost impossible to leave. Elly and Andrew are superb hosts. In no time I was settled on the sofa, drink in hand, happily chatting away as the aromas of dinner preparations built a mouth-watering sense of anticipation. There's something of the English country house about Camerons: frail pine doors and knotted floorboards were through rooms of soft yellow hues. It's smart, but with a wonderful, lived-in feel, to which the collections of cricket bats and Ascot hats, vibrant paintings, brimming bookcases and purposeful antiques all attest. Bedrooms are absurdly comfortable, with blanket boxes and writing tables and access to the garden lawn and azure pool. Outside there's a lushness. Bountiful orchards are swollen with apples, pears, apricots, nectarines, avocados and macadamia nuts. There's the smell of scented roses and twisted eucalypts and the spectacular sight and sound of water running over rock. A two-hundred-foot waterfall virtually plunges to the doorstep. The Camerons run a farm and a winery, housed in a rustic barn built amongst the pines and covered in drooping wisteria. Andrew will guide you around the dusty barrels and Heath Robinson touches that combine to produce an excellent shiraz. The quintessential GG experience.

Rooms: 2: 1 king with en/s shower; 1 king/twin with private shower.
Price: $130 – $160.
Meals: Full breakfast included. Dinner $50 per head which includes drinks.
Directions: Coming north on the Hume Freeway from Melbourne, after 1.5 hours (134km) turn right, signed to Ruffy. Follow signs for Ruffy for 4.6km, then left into Terip Terip Road (gravel) for 2km. Entrance to The Falls is on your right.

Map Number:

Victoria

Delatite Station

Simon Ritchie

Delatite Lane, Mansfield 3722
Tel: 03-5777-3518 Fax: 03-5777-3986
Email: delancy@mansfield.net.au Web: www.delatitestation.com
Cell: 0429-827-292

I passed a large river bearing the name of the station. I then passed a winery, pub and a road that all carry the name. I knew I was getting near! The family's colonial 'run' was 30,000 acres in the 1860s, but today's extant 4250 acres are still wonderful to explore. The homestead is surrounded by exquisite gardens and about the property I came across a rickety old swing-bridge leading to a picnic flat and swimming billabong (a swimabong?), old barns, young racehorses… and the two guest cottages. Bob's has outstanding views of the alpine peaks from a wooden deck, and the living-room floods with morning sun which reflects off deeply polished floors to walls in fresh limes, lavenders and rusty ochres. Chris's Cottage is a sleepy, rustic place, planted between a giant plane tree and the river, which is but a bouquet's fling away. As Single Men's Quarters all the bedrooms open from the verandah, but the bathroom with its giant claw-foot bath connects inside with the living area. An alcove with a fire set behind the grate sets off warm, fuzzy, nostalgic feelings, as does the mantle plank jostling with bottles and candles from nights spent on the benches around the oak table. The gardens are open throughout summer and I bumped into a Ritchie cousin in the rose parterre who was recovering from conquering Everest. *Nearby: skiing, bush-walking, fishing, Lake Eildon, 4WD-ing, exceptional national parks.*

Rooms: 2 Cottages: Bob's has 1 twin, with en/s bathroom; Chris's has 1 double and 2 twins.
Price: From $140 per couple in Chris's, $200 in Bob's.
Meals: At Chris's provisions for your first breakfast are provided. At Bob's you'll find a hamper in the fridge. Restaurants 7 mins drive away.
Directions: From Mansfield head toward Mt Buller, take C511 Jamieson Rd on the right, then go 6km (ignore sign and road to Delatite Winery) and turn left into Delatite Lane. Go 3.6km on dirt road until white picket entrance to Delatite.
Postal Address: Private Bag 1, Mansfield 3722.

Map Number: 5

Erimbali Country Cottage

Jim and Prue Plowman
820 Break O' Day Rd, Glenburn, 3717
Tel: 03-5780-2341 Fax: 03-5780-2238
Email: erimbali@ycs.com.au Web: www.geocities.com/erimbali

This unimprovable hillside cottage used to be a stationmaster's railway cottage until it wa decomissioned, cannily bought by the Plowmans and transported in sections from Yea to i present position, where it gazes down upon the Erimbali garden and farm. Prue will take you, c at least point you off, on walks to hilly vantages about the farm where 360-degree views ar unblemished by man. So the cottage sits, delimited by a rustic fence to keep the nosy black angu cows out of the garden, about half a kilometre from the main homestead in just the right degre of isolation. Waking in the morning was a pleasure, as I peered at the view from the verandal white cockies swooping and screeching, dry summer grass bright yellow in the early morning sur cattle shuffling and snuffling unexpectedly near the house. Mantling breakfast in the huge oper plan kitchen when all the pots and pans are clean, the tomatoes cut, table laid etc is more relaxin than being served. If you can bear to leave Erimbali for the day, there are wineries within twent minutes, the beautiful Yarra Valley, forests and Kinglake National Park. Prue, who is a talented arti and gardener besides her other roles as farmer's wife, mother and hostess, will take you on tour if that's what you want. The charm here is in spades.

Rooms: 1 cottage with 3 double bedrooms with bath and shower in one bathroom.
Price: $150. Weekdays 3 nights for the price of 2.
Meals: Full breakfast included for you to cook yourself.
Directions: From Glenburn take the Break O' Day Rd signed towards Flowerdale for 8.2km – the house is on your right.

Map Number:

The Eltham Garden Retreat

Gwen Ford

70 John St, Eltham 3095
Tel: 03-9439-9010 Fax: 03-9439-9010
Email: fordford@planet.net.au Web: www.elthamgardenretreat.com.au

In all things at Eltham Garden Retreat the emphasis is strongly on the 'natural', whether it be in the building materials used to create the cottages or the garden itself. So you can choose between the sweetest cottage, with exposed mud-brick walls, wooden floor, rugs and furniture in primary colours, or the light-filled loft, a pale, painted-pine studio accessible via a wooden walkway with its own elevated deck. Then there's a Venn diagram of three conjoined adobe rondavels (bedroom, kitchen, sitting-room) with fan-beamed ceilings (if that means anything to you!), whitewashed walls, wicker furniture and a private courtyard garden. These cottages are hidden in the two acres of Australian native bush garden. This amazing slice of wilderness was actually created from an old quince orchard, though you'd never know it. The waterfall and pond are vitally soothing on the eye. In fact I challenge you to find a single object that doesn't blend perfectly into this sylvan environment. Even the wrought-iron lamps – forged at nearby Montsalvat – that land you at your cottage at night are delightfully frayed and antique. A great place from which to visit Melbourne, but also the Yarra Valley wineries, just half an hour's drive from here. And the Yarra River's most beautifully rural areas are within walking distance. Gwen provides breakfast materials for you, putting things she's cooked in your fridge, vegetarians well catered for. An idyll.

Rooms: 3: 2 cottages, both doubles with en-suite shower; 1 loft with en-suite shower.
Price: $120 – $160. Singles $110 – $130.
Meals: Full breakfast included but you need to cook it yourself. Many good restaurants and wineries in Eltham.
Directions: Directions faxed or emailed on booking.

Victoria

Brindalee Cottage

Lynne Vingrys
2 Upper Coonara Rd, Olinda 3788
Tel: 03-9751-1837 Fax: 03-9751-1837
Email: brindaleecottage@hotmail.com
Web: www.geocities.com/Brindaleecottage/

Driving out of Melbourne a sudden elevation takes you beyond the metropolitan basin and u into the dense forest of the Dandenongs. Tucked in amongst strapping mountain ash at the en of a gently winding drive, you'll find Brindalee, a fairy-tale cottage trimmed with blue-grey timbe frames. Under the watchful gaze of scarlet lorikeets, a wrap-around verandah is decorated wit wooden ducks and rocking chairs festooned with woollen throws and crimson cushions. Sittir out here is incredibly peaceful. You enter through a glass door to a borderless living area which when I visited, was warmed by a wood-burner and winter sun. The cottage is delicately furnishe with fabrics: a vibrant patchwork tablecloth, soft blankets, comfy sofas… and more ducks. It Lynne's detailed handiwork that personalises Brindalee: framed embroidery, hand-stencilled wall fresh flower arrangements, wicker baskets full of pine cones and dried lavender. There's a indulgent bathroom where you can share the claw-foot bath with a mop of sponges and bat salts. And the front bedroom has a sleigh bed and access to the bubbling outdoor spa. Should yo manage to pull yourself away, gardens, nurseries and bush walks await. But Lynne assured me th most people don't leave the cottage. *Galleries, potteries and antique shops in Olinda; a golf cours with unrivalled views and the National Rhododendron Gardens are moments away.*

Rooms: 1 self-contained cottage with 2 queens, private bath and shower and separate loo.
Price: $165 – $250 for first couple. Extra people $40 per night each. Single rate available on request.
Meals: Full breakfast ingredients provided.
Directions: From Melbourne take the Burwood Hwy (26) east. At Ferntree Gully turn left onto C415 to Olinda. Follow C406 toward Monbulk. Brindalee on the corner of Upper Coonara Rd.

76

Map Number:

Carlisle

Anne Carlisle

400 Glenferrie Rd, Kooyong, Melbourne 3144
Tel: 03-9822-4847 Fax: 03-9822-6637
Email: carlisle@internex.net.au Web: www.innhouse.com.au/carlisle.html

Anne's home, sequestered behind protective walls in fashionable Kooyong/Toorak, is a find for those who want a truly friendly place to call their own in one of Australia's big smokes. Carlisle is a beautiful 1910 federation home with twelve-foot ceilings, original open fireplaces on angled walls, wide corridors, enormous bedrooms and a large flower garden that is lit up at night. But it is Anne herself, as is always the case with the best B&Bs, who makes your stay special. You don't feel you have to ask before collapsing into one of the sofas or grabbing a book from a shelf… although perhaps you should! Breakfasts are the cherry on the cake, so to speak, with variations such as cheese and chive soufflés, scrambled eggs and chipolatas, omelettes… and the orange juice is freshly squeezed, yes it is. The music system, TV and video etc are at your disposal; pour yourself drinks in the drawing-room (and write them down) and generally make yourself at home. Fergus the dog has an unusual obsession with closing doors, by the way, and spends much of his time stuck (by his own paw) waiting to be saved. *Melbourne's top restaurants, antique shops and sporting facilities are all nearby.*

Rooms: 3: 1 double with en/s shower; 1 double with private bathroom. Also a twin which shares the bathroom if you are travelling in a group.
Price: $140 – $160. Singles full room rate.
Meals: Breakfast included. There are lots of restaurants in the area.
Directions: Directions will be faxed or emailed.

Map Number: 6

Lord Lodge

Jacquie Little
30 Booran Rd, Caulfield 3162
Tel: 03-9572-3969 Fax: 03-9571-5310
Email: lordlodge@aol.com Web: www.lordlodge.com.au

Shielded by 100-year-old Moreton Bay fig trees and surprisingly close to Melbourne's CBD, Lord Lodge sits right on Caulfield Racecourse. The Victorian mansion – designed by Rippon Lea architect, I'm told – also happens to be a fantastic B&B. Inside, rooms named for local champions are vast and extraordinarily detailed: hand-painted cornices and Baltic pine floorboards and the most intricate plasterwork. The sitting-room boasts a rare Champs Elysées-inspired ceiling design. Jacquie is a little dynamo, always looking for things to do. She hand-stenciled those wall panels herself! But however busy she is, she'll always spare time for a chat and fill you in on horse history. You see, first and foremost, Lord Lodge is a racing stable and is steeped in Australian racing history. Built in 1880 when Caulfield racecourse was a snake-infested swamp, its owner decided that a turret would be the safest place from which to watch the track work. Nowadays, you can get much closer to the horses. Before tucking into a "breakfast to die for", watch the misty morning track gallops and pool training or simply wander the old stables. The magnificent barn has a spellbinding presence with its dark wooden walls towering above the sawdust floor. Little wonder that it's featured in many films and that, along with the house, it is listed on the National Estate Register. A thoroughbred through and through.

Rooms: 1 king with en/s shower; 1 queen with en/s shower; 1 double with private bathroom.
Price: $135 – $175. Singles from $115.
Meals: Full breakfast included.
Directions: Lord Lodge is located 10 minutes south of Melbourne's CBD. It is just off Hwy 1 and is close to both the Caulfield and Glenhuntly train stations. The number 67 tram line to the city is 2 blocks away.

Map Number:

Robinsons in the City

Wendy and Jonathan Wright

405 Spencer Street, Melbourne 3003
Tel: 03-9329-2552 Fax: 03-9329-2552
Email: wendyr@alphalink.com.au Web: www.robinsonsinthecity.com.au

For lovers of the boutique B&B, this is Melbourne's Mecca. Wendy ran one of our favourites from the first edition down by the St Kilda shore. She's now moved to another killer location, right in the heart of the city, transfusing Robinsons' charm and style into Melbourne's oldest commercial bakery. Behind the claret brickwork and courtyard, Wendy has arranged her world over two higgledy-piggledy levels, with some stunning original features. Most prominent, of course, are the cavernous bakers' ovens in the breakfast room, dating back to the 1850s. Elsewhere there's a guest pantry with polished brick floor and computer terminal, and a sandy lounge whose giant upholstered sofas are surrounded by books. At one end an iron staircase curls up to the second floor; black Japanese treads lead you back down, beneath a bucket light-shade filled with dead bulbs. The glossy door of your bathroom matches the shower tiles and beside the porcelain bowl you'll find a tiny pumice foot and woven basket of goodies. The colour scheme links bedrooms that are named after Melbournian notables: Spencer, Flinders and Buckley among them. The shuttle from the airport pulls up outside and whichever way you strike out you'll hit a Melbourne monument: Telstra Dome, Queen Victoria Market, Crown Casino, Bourke Mall. The hopelessly romantic colonial tramcar restaurant begins its waltz round the city nearby.

Rooms: 6: 1 king with en-suite shower; 2 kings, 2 queens and 1 twin each with private bathroom.
Price: $175 – $205. Extra person $25 per night.
Meals: Full breakfast included.
Directions: In the heart of Melbourne, Spencer Street runs along the western edge of the CBD grid. Heading north, Robinsons is on the left at the corner with Batman Street, near Flagstaff Gardens.

Bishopsgate House

Margaret Tudball and Ross Bishop

57 Mary Street, St Kilda, Melbourne 3182
Tel: 03-9525-4512 Fax: 03-9525-3024
Email: marg@bishopsgate.com.au Web: www.bishopsgate.com.au

It was pouring with (much-needed) rain when I arrived at Bishopsgate and Marg was concerne
about her guests' Big Day. I felt better off taking tea in her Victorian sitting-room with its imposin
ten-foot gilt mirror, bequeathed by the previous owners, doubtless unwilling to risk bad luck b
moving it. Bishopsgate bears the imprint of Marg's many passions. The Oriental Room reflects he
specialisation in Asian studies; the French Room her francophilia. With its wicker bed, larg
cushions, gilt mirror on an easel and private west-facing sunroom, this is the *choix des amants*. Sh
loves cooking, too, and savvy guests eschew local restaurants in favour of her home-cooke
cuisine. The gazebo in the garden courtyard housed a string quartet and served fine finger foo
during the Melbourne Food and Wine Festival. But it is the many little touches that mak
Bishopsgate special. Wine (from evocative-sounding vineyards) and phone calls are free, guest
are provided with a pouch of Bishopsgate's own aroma-therapeutic toiletries (mine now
commandeered as a rather natty pencil-case) and Marg is quick to offer you a tipple when yo
arrive or a latte from her new coffee-machine. With such hospitality, you knew everything woul
turn out fine for her wedding party. And sure enough, as I left the rain eased and the late afternoo
sun began to break through.

Rooms: 3: 1 king with en/s shower; 1 queen with en/s bath and shower; 1 queen with private shower.
Price: $145 – $215. Apartment on Fitzroy Street (sleeps four) $195 – $250.
Meals: Full breakfast included. Continental breakfast provided in apartment. Lunch ($15 p.p.) and dinner ($25 p.p.) available on request.
Directions: Ask when booking.

Map Number:

Victoria

Fountain Terrace

Penny and Heikki Minkkinen
28 Mary St, St Kilda, Melbourne 3182
Tel: 03-9593-8123 Fax: 03-9593-8696
Email: info@fountainterrace.com.au Web: www.fountainterrace.com.au

Walking up from the beach, I've passed Fountain Terrace many times and each time I've stopped and stared at its grand façade, imagining what elegance lay within. Now I know. As one American guest put it, "it's museum-esque". Chandeliers, ornately-framed prints and chinoiserie have perfectly captured the opulence of the Victorian era. From the Corinthian columned hallway to the butter-yellow and black marble drawing-room the attention to detail is evident in every intricate architrave. Bedrooms are named after Australian luminaries. I stayed in Henry Lawson, a big room with gold and navy brocades. Next door was Nellie Melba, decorated in French blue and white, with private sitting-room and French windows to a wrought-iron balcony. It wasn't always like this. Fountain Terrace was once a boarding house painted in mission brown. Nothing's quite as it seems in St Kilda, which is of course what gives it its charm. As if to prove it, the vivacious Penny invited me along with regular guests for a night out and introduced us to a side of St Kilda I barely knew existed. At the back of a pub I'd normally avoid, I ate authentic goulash amidst thick-set Europeans. Later, we simply walked into what I'd thought was a private house to drink beer with old veterans in a delightfully dilapidated RSL. At breakfast with another set of guests, I concluded that if St Kilda is about shabby chic, then this is the chic bit.

Rooms: 7: 1 king suite with en/s shower and bath; 1 king with en/s spa bath; 2 king and 3 queen with en/s shower.
Price: $165 – $235. Singles $135 – $195.
Meals: Full breakfast included.
Directions: Mary Street runs parallel with Fitzroy Street and sits between Beaconsfield Parade and Canterbury Road.

Map Number: 6

81

Annie's Bed and Breakfast

Ann Briese
93 Park St, St Kilda, Melbourne 3182
Tel: 03-8500-3755 Fax: 03-9534-8705
Email: annies_stkilda@bigpond.com
Web: www.anniesbedandbreakfast.com.au

If you want a slice of the real St Kilda, this is it. Ann (Annie is the name of the house) has been here just long enough to remember life before *Secret Life of Us* put the area on the map again. What she doesn't know about the intrigue, history and characters (past and present) that infuse St Kilda with its bohemian charm probably isn't worth knowing. Here is Melbourne in microcosm. There's an old brass bed brought to Australia by an Englishwoman as her dowry, an authentic Victorian bathroom with claw-foot bath, a rogues' gallery of family members framed in reclaimed wood and a collection of stones from Australia's heartland. Then there's the modern, polished concrete-floored living area, framed with Didier Lourenço prints, with its elevated kitchen from which Ann creates breakfast courses and conducts ensuing discourses. Solid Oregon doors concertina-open onto a brick courtyard populated with sun-loungers, hammocks and fig and lemon trees. I wasn't allowed to leave until I had joined her guests – or were they friends? – in the cosy sitting-room and sampled their Tasmanian cheese. When I finally did leave, I sucked in the invigorating sea air and, armed with Ann's insider know-how, headed to vibrant Acland Street. *Annie's Lane wine sold at cellar-door prices.*

Rooms: 3: 2 queens with en-suite shower; 1 king with private bath with shower above.
Price: $150. Singles $100.
Meals: Full breakfast included. DIY BBQs possible in the courtyard.
Directions: Park Street runs parallel with and one block from Beaconsfield Parade and St Kilda beach.

Map Number:

Redhill Retreat and Cheesery

Trevor and Jan Brandon
81 William Road, Red Hill 3937
Tel: 03-5989-2035 Fax: 03-5989-2427
Email: rhr@alphalink.com.au Web: www.redhillretreat.com.au

An unusual combination I'll grant you, but a tasty one. First and foremost, Redhill is a sylvan retreat where Jan and Trevor have built a rambling, mud-brick home with three guest suites. The bedrooms have slate floors, big beds, pine furniture and glass fronts that open onto private courtyards brightened by Chinese lanterns. Jan will serve you a cooked breakfast here and there's also a BBQ. Stone steps lead past ferns to an orchard with 200 fruit trees – blueberries, citrus, cherries, figs – where you can pick fruit for picnics or really freshly-squeezed juice! There are also eight acres of gum trees on your doorstep, popular with the local koala bear population… and a curious and chummy ring-tailed possum who will keep you company. Perhaps it's the cheese he's after. Trevor used to make cheeses for family picnics. Now he supplies many of the top restaurants in the area. Make sure you try the washed-rind and if you've time he'll show you how to make your own. Mornington Peninsula is littered with beaches and small wineries: the oldest is just across the road. Head to Sorrento for dolphin-spotting or to London Bridge for wonderful views of crashing surf and soaring hang-gliders. Best of all, though, is the drive down to the coast from the top of Arthur's Seat. Of all the roads I've travelled on across Australia, this has to be the most breathtaking, giving an unrivalled panorama of Port Phillip Bay.

Rooms: 3: 1 king with en/s shower; 1 queen with en/s shower and separate bath; 1 family suite with 1 queen, 1 twin and en/s shower.
Price: $180 – $250. Singles $120 – $150.
Meals: Full cooked breakfast.
Directions: Princes Highway (1) then Peninsula Highway (11) to Mornington Pensinsula. Take Red Hill exit left onto Nepean Highway, left again onto White Hill Rd (C787). Right at Arthur's Seat Rd. William Rd on left.

Lilydale House

George and Lit Belcher

100 Dog Rocks Road, Batesford, Geelong 3221
Tel: 03-5276-1302 Fax: 03-5276-1026
Email: belcher@bigpond.com Web: www.innhouse.com.au/lilydale.html

This is a grand old house and George comes from what I suspect is a grand old Geelong family, though he won't thank me for saying it. You'll be hard pressed to find a better welcome in Australia. B&B here is as it should be, in a home with hosts who are happy to see you. George came out to meet me at the car, while Lit put the finishing touches to a delicious roast chicken – she had cooked it in case I was hungry! We ate at the huge blackwood dining table (it seats twelve easily) with a fire smouldering in the grate (as it was at breakfast), and George poured a good red while I counted 35 different bottles on the drinks table. His great-grandfather bought the house as a weekend retreat – 200 acres, ten kilometres north of the city, thus sound-proofing it from all but the birds. Their land runs down to the Moorabool river and roos, platypuses, echidnas, eagles and koalas all visit or live here. If you want to see an Aussie Rules game, Lit and George will take you to see Geelong (if he's not riding his bike from Sydney to Melbourne). There are antiques, a swimming pool and the most comfortable bed in Australia, but it is George and Lit that make the place so special. *Near Anakie Gorge, Geelong and the Botanical Gardens, National Wool Museum, Great Ocean Road.*

Rooms: 3: 1 double and 1 twin, both with en/s shower; 1 double with en/s bath and shower.
Price: $140 – $160. Singles $110 – $130.
Meals: Full breakfast included. Dinner by arrangement, from $45 p.p.
Directions: Leave M1 at Geelong for Ballarat on A300. After about 10km, down hill, over bridge and 1st left into Dog Rocks Rd. Continue 600m and house signed straight ahead at sharp right-hand bend.
Postal Address: PO Box 1700, Geelong 3220.

Elliminook

Peter and Jill Falkiner
585 Warncoort Rd, Birregurra 3242
Tel: 03 5236-2080 Fax: 03-5236-2423
Email: enquiries@elliminook.com.au Web: www.elliminook.com.au

Shades of England in this grand and gracious family home set in 74 acres of sleepy country, only one and a half hours from Melbourne. Jill is delightful and does things instinctively and generously: a fire in the sitting-room, the best linen on old antique half-testers and croquet and tennis in the garden. The house was built in 1865 and has original pine floors and doors running all the way through that give it a very cosy feel. There are tartan sofas in the snug sitting-room, Japanese prints on the walls, rugs on floors and a day bed in the conservatory. Outside, white iceberg roses fill the courtyard and in good weather you can have breakfast there. Big, elegant "country house" bedrooms spoil you all the way. One has an open fire and the original baker's oven. There are ceiling fans, air-conditioners, fresh flowers, good shower rooms and rich fabrics; nothing disappoints. The gardens here are also impressive, with a rich mix of non-native trees and climbing roses that roam at will on the front verandah, but amid all the grandeur of Elliminook it is Jill and her gentle ways that shine most brightly.

Rooms: 4: 2 queens with en/s shower; 2 doubles, 1 with en/s shower and 1 with private spa bath.
Price: $145 – $195. Singles $120 – $160.
Meals: Full breakfast included. Meals available in local restaurants and Birregurra is only 25 minutes from Lorne.
Directions: Travelling west along the M1/A1 turn left to Birregurra. At the T-junction turn right out of Birregurra over small bridge. Elliminook sign-posted, hidden driveway on right. 0.5 km west of town.
Closed: Christmas Day and Boxing Day.

Wanawong

Janet and David Hopkins

950 Colac – Lavers Hill Road, Colac 3249
Tel: 03-5233-8215 Fax: 03-5233-8258
Email: info@wanawong.com.au Web: www.wanawong.com.au

Here's what happened to me at Wanawong. In Apollo Bay, with nowhere to stay, I rang Janet
see if she had a bed for the night. She said she did, sounding delighted at the prospect of havi
me descend on her at the last moment. She met me at the car, showed me to my huge suite
rooms (apologising as if it were a hut), then invited me to join friends and family for dinner. W
pots boiling frantically in the kitchen, she abandoned ship to take me on a tour of the beauti
garden that she and David have expertly reclaimed from the side of the hill on which they bu
their contemporary glass and wood house. Giving me a moment to regain my breath – the vie
here is an awesome sweep across thirty kilometres of forest canopy – she then took me back
the kitchen, where David was waiting with a glass of wine, and effortlessly served a delicio
dinner. In the morning, I had to argue them into letting me pay (by reminding them of why th
do B&B!), and finally, at my car, which I had crashed (somewhat) the night before, I found th
had managed to fix the thing overnight. Did I dream the whole episode and actually sleep ir
ditch that night? I strongly advise you to stay at Wanawong and experience the place f
yourselves.

Rooms: 1 double with en/s bathroom and shower,
with sofa-bed and single in the sitting-room.
Price: $110. Extra people $20 each.
Meals: Continental breakfast included. Lots of
restaurants locally.
Directions: 12km south of Colac on Colac Lavers
Hill Rd (C155), signed on right if heading south. Fro
Great Ocean Rd at Lavers Hill, 12km north of
Gellibrand. Also signed.

Map Number:

Claerwen Retreat

Cornelia Elbrecht and Bill Whittakers

Tuxion Rd, Apollo Bay 3233
Tel: 03-5237-7064 Fax: 03-5237-7054
Email: cornelia_elbrecht@claerwen.com.au Web: www.claerwen.com.au

The track that leads to Claerwen is the start of the adventure. As it winds its way high above Apollo Bay the views are spectacular, but what awaits you at the top is nothing short of magical. Claerwen sits on the highest point in the area and enjoys 360-degree views across ocean and rainforest. On a clear day you can see to King Island, 100km away. At night, the view is no less wondrous, as the sky bursts into a celestial *son-et-lumière*. As stars twinkle above and lights flicker below, there's a sense of being held in a cosmic cradle. Claerwen is a retreat and there's a discreet focus on self-discovery and stress relief. Whether you indulge in one of Cornelia's therapies or not, you'll be lulled by the air of relaxation. It's a stillness that you'll find on your cottage deck overlooking the Otway Ranges and the Great Ocean Road, in the space of your stylish suite or beside the salt-water pool. I found it sunk in the sofa with a book, by the vast free-standing brick fireplace that towers up into the rafters of the open-plan, chalet-style room. And again, in the fern gullies, in a pair of old wellies loaned by Bill, tramping through morning dew and diaphanous mist, listening to the rhythmic ocean swell.

Rooms: 4 rooms in the guesthouse: 1 queen, 2 kings and 1 double twin all with en-suite showers. 2 three-bedroom cottages are also available.
Price: Rooms $200 – $250. Cottages (breakfast not included) $300 – $350.
Meals: Full breakfast included for in-house guests. Cottage guests can have breakfast in the guesthouse at an extra charge or make their own.
Directions: Travelling west, turn right off Great Ocean Road at Mobil garage before Apollo Bay. Continue 6km up road which becomes unsurfaced to top of hill.

Map Number: 6

Spindrift

Ted and Ray Stuckey

2 Marengo Crescent, Marengo, Apollo Bay 3233
Tel: 03-5237-7410 Fax: 03-5237-7410
Email: spindrft@vicnet.net.au Web: www.vicnet.net.au/~spindrft

Ray was insistent, her little place by the sea was too 'downmarket' for us, but I would vigorous
disagree and say that Spindrift is one of the jewels of this book. Ted and Ray run their B&B not
slick professionals, but as the warmest of human beings, greeting their guests as they do family ar
friends (who book in twelve months in advance). What-to-do powwows will draw on the
extensive local knowledge: where to see koalas in the Otway Ranges, the most spectacul
waterfalls to visit, where to eat the freshest seafood in Apollo Bay. Their home – once the
summer house – is a simple, but perfect place to hole up for a few days. Bedrooms have tri
carpets, wicker chairs, comfortable beds, white walls to magnify the light and there are seawa
views through French windows, which lead out to a deck where you can watch the sun rise
the moon shine. The beach is less than 60 metres from your bed and you can snorkel at a re
just 300 metres away. Seals bask here all year round, while dolphins, porpoises and whales a
all passers-by. The view stretches about twenty kilometres across water to Cape Patton and yo
will fall asleep to the sound of the sea.

Rooms: 2 doubles with an extra single; both with
en/s showers.
Price: $100 – $140. Singles $70 – $90.
Meals: Continental breakfast included. Many
restaurants in Apollo Bay.
Directions: Go through Apollo Bay westward with
the beach on the left. Go 1st left and you'll see
Spindrift on your right.

Map Number:

Captain's at the Bay

Robin and Lynne McRae
21 Pascoe Street, Apollo Bay 3233
Tel: 03-5237-6771 Fax: 03-5237-7337
Email: captains@vicnet.net.au Web: www.captains.net.au

Bold angles, bright colours and plenty of windows lend Captain's a breezy beach-house feel. Although Robin and Lynne knocked down the captain's cottage to build their contemporary B&B, he is commemorated in the nautical theme that runs throughout. With shading sails and reclaimed timber, maritime artefacts are used to good effect. There's even a sepia still of the captain himself, standing on the obsolete Apollo Bay pier, part of which now sits solidly above the fireplace. The summery rooms are individually decorated with different hues, hand-picked artwork and fresh flowers. Each of the spotless bed-sitting-rooms have their own access fore and aft, with sliding doors leading onto their own private, planted patios. My favourite was the sunny Loft, with its soaring ceilings, sisal carpeting and crafted staircase, atop of which are two bedrooms, with windows low enough to look out of when you lie in. When you do surface, dive into the famous Captain's breakfast, usually a lively affair with guests trading travellers' tales. Robin and Lynne are consummate hosts, always on hand for a chat or to attend a need. After a full day on the beach, snorkelling, surfing or sunbathing, or in the rainforests walking among the wildlife and waterfalls, you'll be glad to return to the lounge where they'll fix you a drink and let you in on more local secrets.

Rooms: 6: 4 queen-size terrace rooms, 2 with en/s shower, 2 with en/s bath and shower. 1 cottage with queen, en/s shower. 1 loft with 2 queens, private shower.
Price: $188 – $245.
Meals: Full "Australian" breakfast included. Seasonal seafood dinner available in warmer months by arrangement.
Directions: Available by fax or email at time of booking.

Quamby Homestead

John and Jane Murphy
Caramut Rd, Woolsthorpe 3276
Tel: 03-5569-2395 Fax: 03-5569-2244
Email: quambyhomestead@bigpond.com
Web: www.quambyhomestead.com.au

After a long drive in scene-stealing dusk, there's nothing better than to arrive to a warm welcome. Edging through the white picket gate, gravel crunching under foot, I rounded a box-hedge and pulled up at the old pine and iron-lace verandah, where I was greeted by Queen Elizabeth and Princess Margaret – roses, that is. Quamby is awash with them. John and Jane were at the lead-light front door and led me into a grand sitting-room, fire blazing beneath marble mantle, and thrust a welcome beer into my hand. That evening, I was treated to a gastronome's delight and we talked long into the night, before I retired to my "room", an original schoolhouse dating back to the 1840s. You can also stay in the self-contained, weatherboard carriage house or in one of five Mews rooms. On a summer's evening, imbibe the pastoral view from its terrace. Morning brought garden-grown poached pears, which I walked off over the croquet lawn, through orchards, round dams and past a herd of giant, lumbering oaks. With all this, plus the Twelve Apostles, Grampians and Tower Hill, an extinct volcano where I encountered an alarmingly Jurassic emu, on your doorstep, you'll be in no hurry to leave. Heading east or west, you'll pick up useful tips here; John has run tours of both the outback and the MCG. Before buying Quamby, he and Jane were repeatedly drawn back here. Most likely, it'll have the same effect on you.

Rooms: 7: 5 mews rooms and 1 original school-house all with queens and en-suite showers. 1 carriage house with king and single beds and private bathroom.
Price: $130 – $165. Single rate less $10.
Meals: Gourmet cooked breakfast. 3-course dinner with apéritifs, hors d'oeuvres and coffee $40 – $45 per person. Lunch by arrangement.
Directions: From the Great Ocean Rd, Quamby is 32km north of Warrnambool on C171 Caramut Rd. Direct from Melbourne on Hamilton Hwy (3 hours), 20km south of Caramut on C174. Well sign-posted.

Oscar's Waterfront Boutique Hotel

Richard and Sally Douglas
41 Gipps St, Port Fairy 3284
Tel: 03-5568-3022 Fax: 03-5568-3042
Email: info@oscarswaterfront.com Web: www.oscarswaterfront.com

"Bill Bryson came to Port Fairy," the bookseller told me, "but he barely mentions it." Was it forgetfulness or selfishness that he kept this Great Ocean Road anomaly to himself? Suspicions redouble on seeing Oscar's, a magnificent French Provincial hotel rising prominently from its riverside setting. It's clearly the grandest place in town, though discreetly so. I let myself in through a private gate, revealing a lavender-lined courtyard, rose-draped gates, and a sprawl of ivy on the blue-shuttered Belfast Ice Store. Richard greeted me warmly and led me into the stone-tiled hall and up the sweeping staircase to my room, which overlooked the River Moyne. Unpacked and refreshed, I repaired to the drawing-room and, amidst soft rugs and plant prints, nested in a deep armchair with a book and a few choice conversation pieces, in case other guests should join me. Next morning, I walked in salty air past towering pines and the crayfish nets at Fisherman's Wharf, to see the 19th-century lighthouse and mutton birds on Griffiths Island. On return, breakfast had been laid out and, helping myself to a newspaper and coffee, I wandered out onto the waterside verandah. Settling at a marble table, I pored over the news, occasionally taking a moment to appreciate the harmony of distant surf, the clink of sailing masts and slop-and-splosh of the marina, while I awaited my caramelised banana hotcakes. "Eat your heart out, Bryson," I thought.

Rooms: 5 king-size rooms with en/s showers.
Price: $220 – $300.
Meals: Full cooked breakfast included. Choose from à la carte menu prepared by Oscar's chef.
Directions: On entering Port Fairy via Princess Hwy, turn L at Bank St, Port Fairy main street. Follow until you come to a T-jct, turn R into Gipps St. Oscar's is 500m on your left, just past Cox St, and is on river side of Gipps St.
Closed: 23rd to 27th December inclusive.

Victoria

Boroka Downs

Julian and Barbara Carr
Birdswing Rd, Halls Gap 3381
Tel: 03-5356-6243 Fax: 03-5356-6343
Email: enquiries@borokadowns.com.au Web: www.borokadowns.com.au

Barbara and Julian have gone all out to score highly on the wow-ometer… and you might ju
say they've succeeded. For a start the setting is something else: five architect-designed cabi
lazing on a sun-dappled savannah and blending into their surroundings like the grazing kangaroo
before them. Above the clearing loom the viridian peaks of the Grampians, the mountaino
National Park with which the property shares a kilometre-long border. Preserving a harmonio
relationship with these surroundings is paramount for the Carrs who have recently planted 8,00
native trees. Throughout the open-plan, oak-and-glass structure there are stainless-steel fitting
designer furniture, recessed appliances, granite worktops and Italian ceramics, all cann
positioned to make the most of the enthralling natural landscape. A cascade of glass frames th
technicolour vista like a giant cinema screen. No expense has been spared to provide the be
But it's okay, no-one can see you – or so I'm told – so make the most of the Bose sound syster
B&O phone, Loewe TV, Smeg oven and La Cimbali espresso-maker while you can. There's eve
a spare hiking-pack, handy for an energetic romp up Mt Abrupt. When you get back, run a dee
bath, add a drop of essential oil, light a candle and star-gaze, abandoning any ambition to go o
for the evening. A stay here comes with a satisfaction guarantee.

Rooms: 5 'cottages', each with king, circular spa and
walk-in shower.
Price: $395 – $445. Packages available, including an
off-peak, 3-nights-for-the-price-of-2 deal ($795
weekends and $695 midweek).
Meals: A Continental breakfast hamper can be
delivered to your door for an additional $35 per
couple. Good number of restaurants in nearby Halls
Gap.
Take A8 from Melbourne/Adelaide. At
Ararat follow C222 to Pomonal. Travel 5km towards
Halls Gap, turn left onto Birdswing Road at the
signpost. This is 7km south-west of Halls Gap.
Postal Address: PO Box 77, Halls Gap 3381.

92   Map Number:

Tasmania

Corinda's Cottages

Wilmar Bouman and Matthew Ryan
17 Glebe St, Hobart 7000
Tel: 03-6234-1590 Fax: 03-6234-2744
Email: info@corindascottages.com.au Web: www.corindascottages.com.au

Matthew and Wilmar's impeccable taste, which informs every detail at Corinda's, is something to cherish… and perhaps to envy too! The cottages, three converted outbuildings surrounding a Victorian mansion (overlooking Hobart), are filled with period furniture, antique fittings, richly coloured fabrics and fresh flowers. All have original features – wooden beams, convict bricks, pressed-metal ceilings – and interesting histories: the Servants' Quarters pre-dates the house and was built on a convict-run vegetable garden. It also has an inviting little stairway leading to a sitting room under the eaves. The Gardener's Cottage has a cosy bedroom with hand-sawn timber boards, whose narrow gaps let in light and heat from the room below. While the feel is authentic and elegant, you'll not want for modern appliances, which can be conjured up on command. The garden is equally elegant with symmetrical parterres hemmed in by pleached linden trees and English box. It's all tempered with a sense of fun: you'll find a bizarre straw horse, a dressing-up room, a closet shower and a Tasmanian Devil chasing other topiary animals around the garden. It seems the only ones who don't appreciate it are the resident doves, who eschew their beautiful dovecote in favour of Corinda's guttering.

Rooms: 3 self-contained cottages, each with queen bed and shower.
Price: $195 – $220. Long-stay discounts available.
Meals: Continental breakfast provisions included.
Directions: Take Tasman Highway (A3) toward central Hobart. Turn right onto Liverpool Street, loop around roundabout back on yourself and turn left up Aberdeen Street. Corinda's Cottages entrance on left.

Norfolk Bay Convict Station

Dot and Mike Evans

5862 Arthur Highway, Port Arthur 7180
Tel: 03-6250-3487 Fax: 03-6250-3487
Email: evans@convictstation.com Web: www.convictstation.com

This was Australia's first railway station, although the 'train' was convict-powered. It is perhaps a measure of how much fun it was at the Port Arthur penal colony that pushing these goods wagons about was considered a cushy job. The building, built in 1838, has recently been taken over by Dot and Mike whose kitchen is the buzzy heart of the house and a factory for delicious aromas. I sat down to chat just in time to sample my first-ever peanut butter cookies hot from the oven. All the jams are home-made too and the breakfast eggs are fresh, local and a healthy yellow in colour. This is a hands-on B&B where your hosts cook your breakfast on demand and are there to offer assistance and point out the amazing wilderness walks of the area – the peninsula has the highest sea cliffs in Australia, for example. The building sits right by the waters of Norfolk Bay and a creaky wooden jetty demands that you walk out and contemplate the flat mirror of smooth water reflecting hills and boats. In the evening, I recommend you try the slightly mad French café/restaurant in Eaglehawk Neck for wood-fired pizza, and on clear nights here the stars and stillness are awe-inspiring. So much exploration to do in the area and there's always the fascinating Port Arthur penal colony. The night-time tours will put the shivers up you. *The Convict Station is licensed and has a good range of Tasmanian beers and wines.*

Rooms: 5: 1 queen and 2 bunks with en/s shower; 1 double and 1 single with en/s bath; 1 double with en/s bath; 1 twin private sh; 1 queen private shower.
Price: $130 – $150. Singles $90.
Meals: Full breakfast included. Several good restaurants nearby.
Directions: In Taranna signed to right as you come from Hobart.

Millhouse on the Bridge

Suzanne and John Hall
2 Wellington St, Richmond 7025
Tel: 03-6260-2428 Fax: 03-6260-2148
Email: millhouse@millhouse.com.au Web: www.millhouse.com.au

Any vestige of stress left over from airplane flights, long drives or domestic tiffs will evaporate once you are ensconced in Suzanne and John's warm and comfortable realm. Many of their guests do in fact come straight from Hobart airport as Richmond is only fifteen minutes away – I was no exception – and it was uplifting to be welcomed at the door before I could knock and to have a glass of local wine in hand seconds later. The lovely brick-and-sandstone Millhouse was built in 1853 as a steam mill on the Coal River and looks directly onto Australia's oldest bridge. Indeed many of Australia's oldest monuments are in Tasmania, viz St. John's, the oldest Catholic church which is just across the road. Guests can walk along the river or in the gardens and Richmond is awash with heritage buildings. Meanwhile, back at the mill, bedrooms are large, airy, wooden-floored, in warm colours, with big brass beds piled high with pillows and cushions, and they are up several flights of stairs. That this felt unusual shows how long I must have been in Australia where a second floor is a rarity. Breakfast is a lively, altogether affair and Brits were emerging dazed after a long flight just as I was leaving. You are well cared for here and it's a great place to start your holiday in Tassie. No trouble at t' mill.

Rooms: 4: 2 queens and 2 queen/twins; 3 with en/s shower, 1 with private bath/shower. One self-contained cottage for two.
Price: $150 – $185. Singles: full room rate minus $10.
Meals: Full breakfast included. Licensed for wine and other drinks for in-house guests.
Directions: Into Richmond from Hobart (20 minutes away). Follow road through village, go right signed over bridge, the house is immediately on the right.

Map Number: 7

Campania House

Paddy Pearl
Estate Rd, Campania 7026
Tel: 03-6260-4281 Fax: 03-6260-4493
Email: campania@bigpond.com.au

nstructed not to loiter as winter days draw in fast, I arrived at Campania House to be greeted by
a vision in red: the inestimable Paddy Pearl, dressed for dinner. The house is old by Australian
standards (1810) and magnificent by any: a sandstone and cedar building punctured with windows
n a bucolic setting on the trout and-platypus-filled Coal River. It houses a rare cantilevered
staircase and a library littered with manuscripts and book titles announcing historical heroes:
fodder for Paddy's vigorous mind. In the drawing-room, I opened the champagne (with a lady's
sigh) and Paddy recalled the days she spent trawling the world ("every country, bar Chile") as an
itinerant researcher, hitching rides on passing freight ships. Later, we repaired to the dining-room
for a four-course feast round the mahogany table, Paddy presenting dishes as I opened bottles.
We marveled and despaired and postulated until the wee hours of the morning and my hostess,
with Gatlin-gun gusto, reeled off the names and endeavours that birthed Tasmania. At breakfast,
was revived with porridge and stewed rhubarb and scrambled eggs and spinach pancakes and
dispatched with various introductions. I can't recall if the beds were comfy (I fell immediately into
a dreamless sleep) or whether the towels were fluffy (they did the job), but do know that this was
an enlightening experience and one I shan't forget for quite some time. A Tasmanian talisman.

Rooms: 7: 5 doubles (2 have a single bed too), 1 twin and 1
single all sharing 2 bathrooms.
Price: $130 – $140. Singles $90 – $110.
Meals: Full cooked breakfast included.
Directions: From Hobart take the Tasman Highway (A3). At
Cambridge, head north on B31, through Richmond, to
Campania. Turn right in centre of village and follow track to
Campania House on left.

Somercotes

Jan and Robert Riggall

Via Mona Vale Road, Ross 7209
Tel: 03-6381-5231 Fax: 03-6381-5356
Email: somercotes@bigpond.com Web: www.somercotes.com

Now this is the sort of place where you could bury yourself away for a few weeks and sit dov
and write a book. Which is precisely what the lady in the cottage next door was doing. It's t
tranquility, you see: in the simplicity of the whitewashed Georgian cottages, amongst the gums
cherry orchard, or down by the river, fishing for trout. It's also the humbling sense of history th
pervades all the convict-built, National-Trust-listed buildings. Exploring the Ticket-of-Lea
building, Pugmill and Rose cottage, steeped in Riggall family memorabilia, is like stepping back
time. Most remarkable of all is the homestead, with its spiked palisades and window bars
reminder that life on this antipodean Emerald Isle was fraught with danger. Somercotes was
well protected (only one attack breached the embrasures, leaving a bullet lodged in an architrav
that bushrangers were indignant to find such a fortress and Martin Cash complained of meetin:
determination to defend property unbecoming of a gentleman. No such criticism of Jan a
Robert, the sixth generation to live and farm here, your spirited hosts and guides. They pack
me off to my cottage with a basket of freshly-baked bread, then, on remembering the guid
disposition toward freshly-squeezed juice, popped in a couple of oranges! Bury yourself aw
here by all means, but don't miss out on all that Somercotes has to offer.

Rooms: 4 cottages: 2 with double room, 2 with double and tw
rooms; all have showers.
Price: $150 – $165. $25 per extra person. Singles $125 – $13
Meals: Full breakfast provisions provided. Dinner by
arrangement. Prices vary.
Directions: Between Hobart and Launceston on Midland
Highway (A1), Somercotes is 4km south of Ross on Mona Vale
Road, signed to the west. Somercotes sign and entrance
immediately on left.
Postal Address: PO Box 3, Ross 7209.

Map Number:

Franklin Manor

Debbie and Meyjitte Boughenout

The Esplanade, Strahan 7468
Tel: 03-6471-7311 Fax: 03-6471-7267
Email: franklinmanor@bigpond.com Web: www.franklinmanor.com.au

From the breathtaking descent through a denuded lunar landscape, to a laborious haul up Huon pine forest on the Abt railway, there's plenty to do in Strahan: 4WD through the Henty sand dunes, kayak under moonlight, paddling past platypus, or roar out to Hell's Gates by chopper, plane or "wild river jet". It'll all help build an appetite for the main event: Meyjitte's dégustation dinner at Franklin Manor. Meyjitte is a culinary archimage ('a great magician' – this word came through on Word-a-Day this morning!), an inspirational chef and it didn't take much to persuade me to opt for his full-blown 8-course menu, which Debbie introduced course by course: two tongue-tingling trout treatments, smoked eel with fennel jelly in a pineapple parcel and iced vintage Ashgrove cheddar (nothing like you'd imagine!). And then there was carpaccio of scallop: the most delicate and unique taste conceivable. An internationally stocked wine cellar proffers the best vintages; you're invited to browse and select your favourite. The house itself is a grand mansion: large bedroom suites and lounges with window-box seats spilling out cushions. It's also family-run and everyone has a role: the two boys were helping guests in with their luggage when I arrived. Jolly the labrador isn't particularly fussy as to who takes him for a walk. Head out to absorb the endless surf and sunset at Ocean Beach (next stop South America).

Rooms: 14: all queens with mix of en/s spas, baths and showers, plus 4 stable cottages, 2 with a queen and two singles and 2 with two queens and a single.
Price: $185 – $275. No single rate available.
Meals: Continental breakfast included. Dégustation dinner menu available: 4 courses $65 ($85 with wines); 8 courses $85 ($135 with wines).
Directions: Wind down A10 to Queenstown and take B24 to Strahan. In town, turn sharp left to the Esplanade and follow road round harbour. Franklin Manor signed on left.
Closed: August.

Map Number: 7

South Australia

Punters Vineyard Retreat

Sue Hood
Riddoch Highway, Coonawarra 5263
Tel: 08-8737-2007 Fax: 08-8737-3138
Email: punters@coonawarra.lscst.net
Cell: 0407-875-108

This is the stuff of fantasy – a sparkling, architectural dreamscape, surrounded on all sides by flourishing vineyards. When you check in down the road, you can pick up a case of wine, then come up, sit out in the sun and drink of the vines that surround you. The house is contemporary from top to toe, with every tiny detail a monument to cutting-edge design: low-slung wooden beds, walls of glass, galvanised iron, sharp lines, loads of space and a cool, designed feel – expect the best of everything. There is lots of wood, too, in blond ash floors and red gum doors and reclaimed wharf beams which support the house. Slide open one of the huge walls of glass and you can head out for a gentle stroll along avenues of vines. There are no curtains or blinds in the sitting-room, but you won't have visitors here. Then there's a fully-equipped, hi-tech kitchen, a barbecue outside or there are good local restaurants, if you don't want to cook. And if you need any further reason to put Coonawarra on your hit list, Punters Corner won the Jimmy Watson Trophy for Best Red of the Year 2000, Australia's most coveted wine award.

Rooms: 4: 3 queens and 1 king/twin, all with en/s shower.
Price: $210 for two. For each additional couple the price drops, but house only let to one party.
Meals: Full breakfast provided for you to cook. Other meals available at restaurants locally or you can cook or even have a chef come and cook for you.
Directions: Vineyard reception is 3.2km north of Penola on the east side of the Riddoch Highway.
Postal Address: PO Box 296, Coonawarra 5263.

Ann's Place

Ann and George Murphy
2 Royal Crescent, Robe 5276
Tel: 08-8768-2262 Fax: 08-8768-2111
Email: annsplace@bigpond.com Web: www.robesa.com.au/annsplace

Robe is a charming holiday and fishing village with a colourful history full of fishermen and Chinese gold-diggers. Travelling west on the Great Ocean Road, Ann's Place was my first port of call South Australia; it proved an excellent gateway. You really do get well looked after: wonderf baths that run in seconds, big white fluffy towels, excellent beds wrapped up in crisp cotton line and a trim elegance throughout. Ann and George know South Australia inside out, too. A ha hour in their company reveals more about this region than any guide book does. After a although young at heart, they do have a century's experience in the hospitality industry betwee them. Suitably advised, I wandered down to the fishing harbour, where between October an April southern rock lobster are landed every day and where you can buy one freshly cooked fo a beach picnic or dinner back at Ann's. I had arrived out of season, so headed to the Caledonia Inn, a historic pub, where a group of jovial locals insisted that I join them for dinner. In the mornin as both my head and the sea mist cleared, I stepped out onto my patio and, through palm tree and pines, watched jumpy seagulls fossick in Guichen Bay's surf. On warmer days, Ann serves he renowned smoked salmon and scrambled egg breakfast out here. *Great coastal walks and fishin plus 4WD trips over sand dunes. Wineries of the Limestone Coast easily accessible.*

Rooms: 4 queens with en/s bath and shower. Spas 3 units.
Price: $148 – $158. Singles from $140.
Meals: Full breakfast included. Other meals available locally.
Directions: Follow signs off Princes Highway (A1) into Robe. Continue up main street, towards harbour, and house signed 3 doors past Robe Hotel.
Postal Address: PO Box 160, Robe 5276.

Poltalloch Station

Beth and Chris Cowan

Poltalloch Rd, Narrung, Lake Alexandrina 5260
Tel: 08-8574-0043 Fax: 08-8574-0065
Email: info@poltalloch.com.au Web: www.poltalloch.com.au

You can come to Poltalloch for many reasons – the walking, the birdlife, the lake – but chief among its bounties are its history and how beautifully it has been preserved. Poltalloch was one of those big stations of the 1800s, where, if the owner got his sailing boat stuck in the mud 40 miles away (and he did), he sent his minions off to dig it out and carry it back. The mood has mellowed these days, but the past lives on. The smithy, the shearing sheds and the store, all original, survive mostly intact. Beth will proudly show you round, answer your questions and let you explore lost worlds – special indeed. Elsewhere are two flight ponds where much birdlife gathers, low hills with clumps of gum trees and Lake Alexandrina (Australia's largest), gateway to the Murray. You can swim from the beach and at the boathouse you'll find surf skis and rowing boats. Alternatively, arrive under sail and moor here. You can stay in various places – Beth will help you choose. The old farm buildings have been renovated in keeping with the place. Don't expect anything too fancy, but if you like the sound of a snug, romantic cottage, woodburners, stone chimneys, sisal matting and crimson sunsets over the lake, you'll be in heaven. *Coorong National Park is very close, a spectacular wetland – local guided tours can be arranged.*

Rooms: 3 cottages: 2 with 2 (1 double & 1 twin) bedrooms; 1 with 4 bedrooms and 2 bathrooms.
Price: $140 – $190. Lower rates available without breakfast.
Meals: Breakfast provisions provided for you to cook. Evening meals available by arrangement. Alternatively, self-catering or local restaurants (20 mins). BBQ.
Directions: From Meningie travel north on Princes Highway for 20km. L at Narrung turn-off. Poltalloch 10km down track, signed on L. From Tailem Bend, Narrung turn-off is 28km south, before Ashville.
Postal Address: P.M.B. 3, Narrung via Tailem Bend 5260.

Map Number: 8

Portee Station

Ian, Margaret and Susan Clark
Portee Station Road, Blanchetown 5357
Tel: 08-8540-5211 Fax: 08-8540-5016
Email: portee@portee.com.au Web: www.portee.com.au

One of the most extraordinary aspects of Australian life is the tense relationship between Man and Land, and the resilience of both. Nowhere is this more apparent than at Portee Station, and a sta... here is an adventurous outback education. The classic pastoral homestead is built of loc... limestone with corrugated-iron roof, wrap-around verandah and separate kitchen and dining room. Large bedrooms run off a spinal hallway and spill onto a sloping lawn that runs down t... the 1,000-year-old gums lining Portee Creek. It teems with colourful flowers and birdlife and ... summer Susan will prepare a fabulous farm-supplied banquet to eat out on the lawn. You ca... easily visit the Germanic villages of the Barossa from here or join Ian in his boat to check yabb... pots, look for Aboriginal settlements and stop off for a cooling dip as you weave up waterways t... the mighty Murray. But these wetlands quickly give way to desiccated mallee scrub, plagued b... salination, drought and pests. This is where you'll get a hands-on lesson in station life. There's ... de-sanitised tour of the drafting, mulesing and shearing facilities, where legendary shearers c... their fleece. You can also help muster sheep or go spotlighting for hairy-nosed wombats. As I le... Ian was preparing his jalopy to scour Portee's 40,000 acres for sheep, shearing day looming. '... you're still here then," he said, "you'll be given a job." A surprisingly tempting offer.

Rooms: 8: 4 queens with additional single beds, 2 queens and 2 twins all with en/s bath and shower.
Price: $224 (B&B) – $518 (all meals, accommmodation and guided tour). Single rate $161 – $365.
Meals: Full breakfast included in B&B price, more meals included in higher prices. Individually, 3-course dinner (without wine): $44 p.p. Lunch: $29 p.p.
Directions: From Adelaide, follow the Sturt Highway (A20) to Blanchetown. Turn right at the BP station and right again onto a track signed to Swan Reach. Portee signed on right.
Postal Address: PO Box 320, Blanchetown 5357.

Al-Ru Farm

Ruth and Alan Irving
One Tree Hill Rd, One Tree Hill 5114
Tel: 08-8280-7353 Fax: 08-8280-7544
Email: ruthirving@hotmail.com Web: www.ruthirving.com.au

Ruth and Alan entertain generously and their home is so relaxing and beautiful that friends tend to move in. However, the gardens here are so spectacular that they deserve special praise. Ruth has spent the last 20 years creating what must be one of the finest private house gardens in Australia. It has been featured in countless magazines and has appeared in the odd coffee-table book. I am no expert and hardly know a daff from a tulip, but meandering around with Ruth, my jaw well and truly dropped. This was one of the highlights of my trip to South Australia. In the six acres of country gardens you will come across a thousand roses, a substantial lily pond, a 40-foot tunnel of wisteria and, including Ruth, three gardeners. Incredibly, she also finds the time to buy and sell antiques, while Alan, a vet, keeps the local cats and dogs in shape. A lady popped in to report two stray dogs while we were having tea. And the firewood delivery arrived at the same time. Ruth handled us all with natural charm and practised calm. And they say these country people have quiet lives! Stay in a private suite in the Irvings' house or, for the romantic, the Garden Pavilion has its own private garden. Half an hour takes you to Adelaide city or the Barossa wine region, making Al-Ru an excellent base for South Australian explorations.

Rooms: 3: Garden Pavilion (own garden, self-catering) with 1 queen with en/s bath/shower; in the house 2 kings and 1 double (same party) sharing shower.
Price: Garden Pavilion $220 for first night, $110 per night thereafter. In-house $110 – $125 per couple.
Meals: Full breakfast included. Dinner, 2 courses $30, 3 courses $40 (includes coffee and wine), by arrangement.
Directions: Easy to find. Ask for details when booking.

103

Lawley Farm

Lesley and Jack Gregg
Krondorf Rd, Tanunda 5352
Tel: 08-8563-2141 Fax: 08-8563-2141
Email: lawleyfarm@ozemail.com.au Web: www.lawleyfarm.com.au
Cell: 0403-156-403

This is the epicentre of the Barossa with Jacob's Creek – the actual creek, that is – passing by about 100 metres from the front door. Better still, the house is surrounded on all sides by vineyards that produce grapes for three of South Australia's finest: Rockford's, Charles Melton and Trevor Jones. Jack and Lesley have 17 acres of vineyards of their own, which supply the aformentioned luminaries and you are welcome to stroll around or lend a hand. Alternatively, they can arrange for you to visit the cellars for tastings. The settlement here goes back to 1851 and the beautiful converted barns and stables where you sleep have kept their original beams, fireplaces, stone floors and high ceilings. There are wicker chairs on the verandah outside each room, while inside you'll find rugs, brass beds, ceiling fans and good bathrooms. Breakfast comes to you on trays and you can choose from a long list of cooked delights: eggs Benedict, fresh herb omelettes, or smoked salmon and scrambled eggs. When you've eaten, you can walk to the end of the garden and thank the chooks. On your way down you'll pass fruit trees – apple, pear, orange, grapefruit and lemon – and Wellington the dog.

Rooms: 4: 3 doubles and 1 double with single annex; 2 with en/s showers and 2 with en/s showers and spa baths.
Price: $165 – $215. Singles available.
Meals: Full breakfast included. Other meals available locally.
Directions: From Tanunda south for Lyndoch for about 4km, then left, signed Lawley Farm – 1km on left.
Postal Address: PO Box 103, Tanunda 5352

Map Number:

Jacob's Creek Retreat

Wyndham and Patricia House

Nitschke Road, Tanunda 5352
Tel: 08-8563-1123 Fax: 08-8563-0727
Email: jacobscreek@bigpond.com.au Web: www.jacobscreekretreat.com.au
Cell: 0403-870-426

Sweeping through mottled vines to Provençal pencil pines, walled gardens and espaliered olives, you'd be forgiven for thinking you'd ventured into a rustic French village. Raked courtyards and gravel tributaries lead to a cluster of simple, blue-stone cottages. Inside, the wood-floored rooms are gorgeous, with elegant sitting-rooms and king-sized beds, plump with feather eiderdowns and piles of pillows. Some have kitchens, others sun rooms and all have log fires and country-style antiques spilling onto sunny verandahs. You'll soon be seduced onto an enchanting lawn peppered with agapanthus, to play pétanque or laze in a hammock strung between gum trees, or just to dip your feet in the cooling creek at the end of garden, serenaded by birdsong on the breeze. The setting is an undeniable idyll, but the real draw card here is the food. Wyndham is a classically trained chef who has cooked the world over. He'll present you with an individually tailored, 8-course dégustation menu, perfectly married with wine sourced from those hidden wineries that tourists never seem to find. Best of all, you can eat wherever you want. Patricia will set up a table in the privacy of your own suite or in one of the inner courtyards. You may prefer to eat amongst the David Austen roses or, most magical of all, in twilight by Jacob's Creek itself.

Rooms: 5 kings with en/s spa and shower.
Price: $240 – $315.
Meals: Full breakfast included; supplied as farm produce to 3 rooms and delivered cooked to other 2. Dégustation dinner menu available: $70 – $165 p.p.
Directions: From Adelaide, take B19 at Gawler, passing through Lyndoch toward Tanunda. Over Jacob's Creek, turn right down Kock Rd and right again into Nitschke Rd, to the end.
Postal Address: PO Box 599, Tanunda 5352.

The Miner's Cottage

Brenda and Godfrey Gardiner
Cockatoo Valley, Barossa Valley 5351
Tel: 08-8524-6213 Fax: 08-8524-6650
Email: miners@koalaair.com.au Web: www.minerscottage.com.au
Cell: 0419-806-262

I can only assume that the miner struck gold! This is a perfect synthesis of natural landscape, styli
design, brilliant renovation and delightful hosts. The inside is ravishing, with white-washed wal
crisp linen, piles of cushions, dried lavender and rosemary on racks... even a Christmas tree
December. It's small and snug, extremely romantic and it just gets better (which is sayi
something) when you walk out back to your private verandah and find lush views along Yak
Creek through tall, shimmering gum trees. Kangaroos come in to drink, cockatoos fly by, so gr
the binoculars and sit out back for an hour or two, watching life go by. You can stroll down to th
pool for a swim or keep going and walk around the 66 acres that cocoon you. There are hea
of old gold mines on one side or you can strike out for the reservoir on the other. By day th
Barossa and its wineries are on your doorstep or, if you want more adventure, Godfrey is a pil
and runs day tours up into the Flinders and the outback beyond – a great way to see this beauti
state. Perfect. *Barossa goldfields walk, winery cellar door tastings, cooking schools, ballooning, glidin*

Rooms: 1 cottage with 1 double (and a sofa bed for
children).
Price: $165. Weekends 2-night minimum.
Meals: Full breakfast included. BBQ packs and picni
hampers provided.
Directions: South through Cockatoo Valley and
Goldfields Rd. 1st right (500m) then immediately left
Signed left after 1.2km.
Postal Address: PO Box 28, Cockatoo Valley
5351.

Map Number:

Wisteria Terrace

Ann Schioldann
26 Blackburn Street, Adelaide 5000
Tel: 08-8364-5437
Fax: 08-8364-6961
Email:
stay@adelaideoldterraces.com.au
Web:
www.adelaideoldterraces.com.au

Squeezed picturesquely between ocean and hills, Adelaide is a sedate city, pleasingly plotted with cathedrals, parks and regal stone terraces. It is also extremely friendly and open-minded, with a burgeoning artistic community. Wildlife, water, wickets and wine are all at hand. You can stroll around town and visit its edifying museums, jump on a tram and rattle down to Glenelg beach for the day, or head for the Torrens River, which sweeps through the heart of the city. Whatever you do, Ann has just the place to stay. She is something of a traveller and her four very pretty (and very central) terraced houses are full of Indian and Indonesian furniture picked up on trips abroad. One has an inviting timber sleigh bed and painted balcony, below which the colonial tram quietly trundles. Others hold carved Indian wood, collections of Javanese hats and all have pretty oriental fabrics. There's much contemporary Australian comfort, too, with an open-plan feel, sisal rugs on polished wood floors, maybe terracotta tiles in the kitchen, the sunken bath and cedar-wood blinds in a glass-roofed bathroom, your modesty thoughtfully preserved with a canopy of wisteria. And you get an entire house to yourself, which is good value indeed. A generous Continental breakfast is left in the fridge, although Ann spoke enthusiastically of a local flower shop that doubles as a café, so you may like to try that instead.

Rooms: 3: 1 house sleeping 7, 1 cottage sleeping 4 and 1 apartment sleeping 2.
Price: $140 – $200. $35 – $40 per additional person per night. Minimum 2 nights. Longer stays are cheaper.
Meals: Continental breakfast provisions provided. Self-catering available for other meals or there are restaurants nearby.
Directions: Provided on booking.

Stranraer Homestead

Lyn and Graham Wheaton

Wheaton Rd, Macgillivray, Kangaroo Island 5223
Tel: 08-8553-8235 Fax: 08-8553-8226
Email: stranraer@kin.net.au Web: www.stranraer.com.au

Sitting in the mist of Kangaroo Island's extraordinary natural beauty is this rather grand 3,000-acr farm. Having navigated past penguins and kangaroos (where else will you do this outside a zoo? I arrived to be greeted by Graham, who ensured I was settled in before joining other guests fo a sumptuous dinner. You need to know that Lyn is a fantastic chef and runs cooking courses c the island. Stranraer is the Wheaton family home, always has been. It was Graham's father wh established the property back in 1911 and he who put in the cricket oval. As farming clearly ru in Graham's blood, so does hospitality in Lyn's. She presides over Stranraer, keeping the plac spic-and-span, with lots of homely comforts and fine cooking (she likes to use the excelle Kangaroo Island produce wherever possible). Bedrooms have big brass beds, ornate fireplace high, plaster-moulded ceilings and thick rugs on wooden floors – all very comfortable – and bi original, wooden window-frames that flood the rooms with light. Bathrooms, instead of bein small and en-suite, are big and next-door, with cast-iron baths, screens, wooden blinds, plants ar smart tiles. Breakfast is the biggest imaginable. Close by you'll find the beach at D'Estress Bay c stay at home and wander the farm. There are two large lagoons where a rich and varied birdli gathers. A very peaceful spot and the Wheatons' warm hospitality is second to none.

Rooms: 3 doubles, all with their own bathrooms.
Price: $170 – $195. Singles $130 – $150.
Meals: Full breakfast included. 3-course dinner by arrangement: $48 per person. Lunch and tea hampe (including wine): $30 per person.
Directions: Going west from Penneshaw, pass the American River turn, then 2km and left, 11km to T-junction and left for 4km. Signed right up Wheaton Road.
Postal Address: PO Box 30, Kingscote 5223.

Map Number:

Thorn Park Country House

David Hay and Michael Speers

College Rd, Sevenhill via Clare 5453
Tel: 08-8843-4304 Fax: 08-8843-4296
Email: stay@thornpark.com.au Web: www.thornpark.com.au

As no one else was staying on the night I visited, we sat in the kitchen drinking Brother John's fabulous wines. David said he wasn't cooking anything special in my honour, but David is a liar and he produced the best meal I ate in South Australia – pasta putanesca, a sweet and delicious mix of olive, garlic, onion, chilli, oregano and tomato. Such is the spirit of Thorn Park. Dating from the 1850s, it's a grand place, beautifully furnished with glittering antiques and it stands in sixty acres of majestic country... but it's utterly down-to-earth and very relaxing, too. No airs and graces, but everything is done perfectly and David and Michael have rightly built up a reputation for running the best place to stay in the state – which I think it is. Wander the grounds and you'll find wild olive trees, a riot of lavender and the church of St Aloysius (where Brother John makes his wine). Inside: coir matting, delicious bedrooms, a clipped English elegance and French windows that give onto vine-shaded verandahs. Breakfast was supreme, the highlight an ambrosial roasted nut muesli 'drizzled' with local honey. The Clare valley cradles the property and the Riesling cycle trail runs past 24 vineyards; you can hire bikes in town. We really suffered in trying to choose just two photos for the guide. Tremendous.

Rooms: 6: 3 queens in the house, all with showers. 2 individual coach-house queens, 1 with bath, 1 with shower. 1 self-contained flat in Tuscan-style barn.
Price: $325. Singles from $225.
Meals: Full breakfast included. 3-course dinner available from $65 p.p.
Directions: In Sevenhill (7km south of Clare) take College Rd (west) for 1.25km where you will see a sign to Thorn Park.
Postal Address: PO Box 63, Sevenhill, via Clare 5453.

North Bundaleer

Marianne and Malcolm Booth

Spalding Road, Jamestown
5491
Tel: 08-8665-4024
Fax: 08-8665-4080
Email:
stay@northbundaleer.com.au
Web:
www.northbundaleer.com.au

Built in 1901 as a display of wealth, North Bundaleer lay in a state of disrepair until the Booth came along to restore its opulent glory. The result is stunning, from the Arts and Crafts Movement hallway to an ornate ballroom lined with hand-painted, Lincrusta wallpaper and burled walnut door-panels. The sitting-room is a stately synthesis of Corinthian columns, intricate rugs and crystal chandeliers. The dining-room houses a formidable Irish Georgian table where Marianne hosts convivial dinner parties. The bedrooms are breathtaking, particularly the Red Room: cotton damask canopy bed, spot muslin drapes and damask pillows. This one has its own sitting-room and the most exquisite bathroom, an entire conservatory devoted to translucent ablutions. I could all be a little overwhelming if it wasn't for Marianne and Malcolm's down-to-earth style. They encourage you to use the house as your own. Marianne is a pedigree hostess and a love of entertaining courses through her veins. She was keen to show me where guests are whisked for picnics and sundowners. We bounced past cows and chickens, blue gums and creek beds, up to a hilltop panorama surveying pastures, plantations and the majesty of a troop of euros in full flight (that's kangaroos, not Belgians). When we returned, she whipped up a sublime omelette and invited the neighbouring farmer to join us. *Clare Valley tours, ballooning, 4WD and scenic flights*

Rooms: 4: 3 queens with en/s bath and shower; 1 king with private shower.
Price: $180 – $280 per person. Single rate $250 – $350. Rate includes all food and drink.
Meals: Full cooked breakfast and 4-course dinner with wine and coffee included in tariff. Lunch or picnic hamper with wine: $30 per person.
Directions: Leaving Clare take right fork (83) to Jamestown, turning left at Spalding. Head north 22km to pine plantation. At Jamestown sign continue 2.4km. Turn at "Pegasus" sign on right.
Postal Address: PO Box 255, Jamestown 5491.

Map Number: 8

Explore the Outback Camel Safaris

Phil and Ifeta Gee

PMB 118 William Creek, Via Port Augusta 5710
Tel: 08-8672-3968 / Freecall in Oz 1800-064-244 Fax: 08-8672-3990
Email: explore@austcamel.com.au
Web: www.austcamel.com.au/explore.htm

A brilliant dawn draws me from my swag. I have a camel to look after (or is that vice versa?) and, hobbling his feet, I realize that camels are the largest animal that I'll ever handle. Later, I walk out to shepherd their short-step grazing: a futile task. Back at camp, the morning ritual begins. Under Phil's watchful gaze, we buckle girths and clip sacks to saddles in sequence. We fumble over intricate knots barely learned, our cuddly dromedaries silently suffering us. Then we're off, at a relaxed pace, alternately walking and riding – Phil leads the string on foot. Inquisitive eagles and intermingled red and grey kangaroos watch from a distance; unthreatened, a perenti lizard waits patiently for us to pass. We're following the path of the Overland Telegraph Line and come across the ruins of a copper mine, an artesian spring and a bore to swim in. By mid-afternoon we've made camp and gather firewood to get the billy boiling. As the sun smears the sky, we huddle round the campfire, nursing wine, and listen to Phil's cracking tales. This is a unique opportunity to experience the outback in safe hands. Phil and Ifeta have been researching the Lake Eyre basin for 15 years. Join them on their next expedition and let some of their passion for camels and knowledge of this country rub off on you.

Rooms: Swag (canvas bedroll with mattress), sheets and pillows provided. If you don't have your own sleeping bag, you can borrow one. No en-suites!
Price: $756 p.p. for 4 days (Thurs p.m. – Mon a.m.). Everything (meals, wine, swag, insurance) incl'd. 15% – 20% less for families, students, OAPs.
Meals: All meals included in price. Vegetarian menu available.

Directions: By car: Stuart Highway to Coober Pedy, then across to William Creek. North from William Creek to Warrina. The Outback Mail Run can take you from Oodnadatta or Coober Pedy. Check with Ifeta.
Closed: 1st November – 31st March.

Western Australia

Craythorne Country House

Julie and Ken Poultney

Worgan Road, Metricup 6280
Tel: 08-9755-7477 Fax: 08-9755-7477
Email: craythorne@netserv.net.au Web: www.craythorne.com.au
Cell: 0419-043-432

It's moments like this that make mine such a good job. In glorious countryside, I trundle up a jarrah-lined avenue, dappled by winter sun, to a shielded homestead. On a cushioned bench, a stretched-out cat is oblivious to chicks exploring the garden's undergrowth. I let myself in to the entrance hall, whereupon I'm greeted with spicy smells of home-made chutneys, pickles and jams, the warm smiles of my hosts and an invitation to join them for lunch. Ken and Julie claim that, compared to other businesses they've run, this is a breeze. They certainly make it look that way. Bedrooms are large and uncomplicated: a comfy bed, fridge for wine and a private patio. The garden here is perennially colourful with lilac diosmas, lavender and rose parterres. There's a dam surrounded by red gums and weeping willows and paddocks where kangaroos congregate. At the back, a croquet lawn is trimmed with azaleas. On the verandah, canvas chairs saddled with glossy magazines – Wine, Decanter, Gourmet Traveller – are silent reminders that you're in wine country. After breakfast, waddle off to a winery: Evans & Tate, Vasse Felix and Moss Wood are clustered close by. Craythorne is a farm and turkeys, ponies, alpacas and chooks roam free. Some city slickers become so taken with the animals that Julie does a roll-call when they've left.

Rooms: 4 queens with en/s shower.
Price: $110 – $150. Single rate available on request.
Meals: Full cooked breakfast included. Dinner menu available including gourmet platter ($30 for two), quiche ($10 p.p.), soup ($5 p.p.) and cake ($5 p.p.).
Directions: From Busselton take Bussell Highway toward Margaret River. North of Cowaramup, Worgan Road is on left. Follow track to Craythorne signed on right.
Postal Address: PO Box 286, Cowaramup 6284.

Wildwood Valley

Anne Sargent
Wildwood Rd, Yallingup 6282
Tel: 08-9755-2120 Fax: 08-9755-2120
Email: stay@wildwoodvalley.com.au Web: www.wildwoodvalley.com.au

Most visitors to Perth will make their way down to the Margaret River area to visit the wineries and then think about where to stay. I'd reverse the process, stay at wonderful, woods-bound Wildwood Valley and then think about what to do! Anne built the house fifteen years ago, with lots of wood, a first-floor verandah from which you can see the sea and views down the eponymous valley. There are 120 acres of woods, fields, sheep, kangaroos and horses (it's mainly a stud). The bedrooms concentrate on great beds and linen; there's a full-size snooker table, a video library, a large sitting-room with real fires in winter and a heavenly gazebo, sometimes the breakfast venue. Anne herself is amazing: not just a great hostess, but also a farmer, a nurse, a cook and a campaigner fighting to keep the developers off the pristine beaches. And she cares for sick kangaroos, most time-consumingly of all. When I visited, Baby Roo was being bottle-fed and was allowed a quick lollop around the sitting-room before retiring back to her basket. Anne says that she usually has an orphan in tow, but it is not guaranteed. Breakfasts are always eaten together, a chance for guests to chat and to meet Anne. This book is all about atmosphere, character and people. And so is Wildwood Valley.

Rooms: 8: 5 B&B rooms, all en suite, 1 self-contained apartment with 2 bedrooms, 1 bath & 1 shower, & 2 x 3-bedroom self-contained cottages each with 2 bathrooms.
Price: $145 – $195. Singles less $20. Cottages $180 – $225 for two people, additional people $25. Apartment $180 – $225 for up to five people.
Meals: Full breakfast included for in-house guests. Continental breakfast provisions supplied for cottages on first morning if requested.
Directions: Take Caves Road (10) to Dunsborough following signs to city centre. Pass McDonalds and on to Dunsborough Lakes. Left at roundabout, continue 8km to T-junction. Turn right, Wildwood Valley 2km on left.

Map Number: 9

Fothergills of Fremantle

Anne and Tony Robertson and David Cooke

20-22 Ord St, Fremantle, 6160
Tel: 08-9335-6784 Fax: 08-9430-7789
Email: fothergills@iinet.net.au Web: www.babs.com.au/fothergills

The summery, seaside-of-old feel at Fothergills instantly appealed; so too its painted deckchairs that adorn the walls. They're auctioned off to support the local theatre and David has a collection to rival London's Hyde Park. The work of mainly local artists, they add another layer of fun to an already colourful house teeming with the artists' other efforts: paintings, sculptures, woodwork and glass. A tiled hallway leads into the brightest of kitchens with jarrah floorboards and a granite-topped island around which you can join Anne for mid-morning coffee. Breakfast is served in a sunroom with limestone walls and a wave of glass that curls round the room. Antique Indonesian (talking) pieces get guests guessing. Upstairs, the bedrooms remember two of Fremantle's finest: Holdsworth, a convict-made-good; O'Connor, the engineer responsible for the harbour this bedroom overlooks. The cream-and-blue Endeavour room invokes the elegance of Captain Cook's ship. Its reproduction Regency furniture includes a lit bateau, cabriole-legged chair and chest with a specimen drawer. At the other end, the hall leads onto a delicate iron lace balcony, populated with wicker and wood. From here you can see Rottnest Island. David is described as an eccentric surgeon, but I think he keeps the two identities separate: out of scrubs, he'll don his driving bonnet and run guests down to the beach in his Morris Minor Tourer. Fantastic.

Rooms: 3: 1 king/twin and 2 queens, all with en-suite shower.
Price: $130 – $170. Singles less 10% (in off-season only).
Meals: Full breakfast included.
Directions: From Perth follow signs to Fremantle. Take Queen Victoria Street over Fremantle Bridge and turn right at T-junction. At roundabout, left into James Street becoming Ord Street. Fothergills on left.

Possum Creek Lodge

Helen and Leon English

6 Lenori Rd, Gooseberry Hill, Perth 6076
Tel: 08-9257-1927 Fax: 08-6293-1627
Email: possum@git.com.au Web: www.possumcreeklodge.com

First it was Chinese gardeners growing gooseberries, then came weekenders hauled up on a zig zag railway, which brought prized jarrah wood back down the hill. Now the wild bush an cultivated vineyards of Perth Hills are at your disposal too. Possum Creek has a trio of homestea suites, one of which has a distinctly Italian feel with Medici artwork and a Tuscan courtyard. I wa in the bright, summery cottage opposite and felt immediately at home. What a relaxant, after long flight, to be able to privately potter, make a cup of tea, settle on the sofa and flick throug magazines and TV channels. It helped that I'd arrived to such a warm welcome from Helen. Sh was busy organising the local Spring Garden Festival and her garden's lush and colourful plar were helpfully name-tagged with trademark attention to detail. Leon popped by and we strolle amongst the interconnected patios, ponds and footbridges and discussed the river tours he ru up and down the Swan River in a 1950s classic timber boat. I returned to contemplate dinne On my doorstep was all I needed: doctor, deli, butcher, restaurant and bottle-shop, as well as patisserie whose reputation stretches across Perth. On Sundays, the place is abuzz with cyclis from Fremantle. I sat down to a wood-fired pizza on my north-facing balcony and watched th setting sun paint Perth pink.

Rooms: 5 self-contained apartments: 3 studios with queen bed, en/s shower and kitchen; 2 suites with queen beds and second bedroom, one with en/s spa one with en/s shower.
Price: $155 – $195. Longer stay packages available.
Meals: Generous breakfast provisions provided on first morning. Cooked breakfast delivered to room from $8.50 – $11. Restaurant and deli across road.
Directions: Perth Hills 15 mins east of airport. Fror Roe Highway, take Kalamunda Rd, turn left into Zam Rd, then right turn into Lenori Rd.

Map Number:

Rosemoore

Shelley Rose
2 Winifred St, Mosman Park, Perth 6012
Tel: 08-9384-8214 Fax: 08-9385-6373
Email: rosemoore@bigpond.com Web: www.rosemoore.com.au

Shelley's family owns a farm in the south-west and there is a good deal of the countryside about this town residence, with chickens at the end of the garden and a cockateil in a cage. It's a simple arrangement, three rooms lined up along a verandah looking inwards to the garden, and I instantly warmed to the place. Shelley is a natural and easy-going hostess and the bedrooms are prettily furnished in country style with wooden floors, doors and decks, brass beds, wicker chairs, gingham table cloths, a rustic dresser and each room has one ecclesiastical stained-glass window that looks streetwards and double doors out to the verandah. All the rooms have en suite bathrooms, TVs, tea and coffee, heaters, electric blankets, ceiling fans and air-conditioning, and access is private from the off-street parking at the side of the property. Guests gather on the wooden deck outside the cottage for outdoor breakfasts... cooked to order and lots of fresh fruit (grapefruit and eggs come from the family farm). Rosemoore is well placed for Fremantle, and Cottesloe Beach is a 2-minute drive away – or you can use the house bicycles. Restaurants can be walked to and I had a delicious meal at the Japanese restaurant round the corner. A B&B with a nice, cosy atmosphere.

Rooms: 3: 1 queen/twin with en/s bath; 2 queens with en/s shower.
Price: $100 – $110. Singles $80 – $90.
Meals: Full breakfast included. Restaurants walkable distance.
Directions: Ask when booking.

Caesia House

Jane and David Tucker
32 Thomas St, Nedlands, Perth 6009
Tel: 08-9389-8174 Fax: 08-9389-8173
Email: tuckers@iinet.net.au Web: www.caesiahouse.com

I know it's a cliché, but this really is an oasis in the city. Nedlands is a leafy suburb tucked between the bustle of Perth, the cafés and clothes shops of Subiaco and the breeze-blown boa on Swan River. The house is a modern villa fronted by the Caesia tree and a hapless macadami perennially under attack from white-tailed black cockatoos (Hitchcockatoos?). Bedrooms hav private access, while the pale-green lounge, all set about with ancestral antiques, is a relaxing plac to enjoy a bottle of wine from the fridge… and there are games, a TV and a library of books t enjoy there too. The elevated dining-room, meanwhile, looks onto the palm-treed garden. Whi the emphasis inside is on cooling and calming, outside is a kaleidoscope of colour. The bright-re coral tree attracts a pandemonium of parrots and a bottle-brush weeps over the swimming poo On fine days – most are – breakfast is served out here, under the shade of a vine-clad canop Jane makes your stay tailor-made and will advise on varied local eateries within walking distanc Before dinner, walk off your jetlag through the manicured university grounds and watch dolphir play in Matilda Bay. Jane is also a guide for King's Park, 1,000 acres of parkland bursting wit wildflowers in spring. *Venture to Cottesloe Beach, the new Maritime Museum, Subiaco Stadium, th WACA, the aquarium and zoo; 15 mins by bus to Fremantle, 10 to the City.*

Rooms: 2: king (twin) and queen, both with en/s shower.
Price: $100 – $130. Singles $95 – $115.
Meals: Continental breakfast with fresh/poached fruits and yoghurt included. Hot breakfast $9 p.p. Other meals available on request from $30 p.p.
Directions: 7 mins from Perth CBD, follow Stirling Highway signs via Mounts Bay Road. On Stirling Highway pass university. Thomas Street on left at top of rise. Caesia House on left.

Hope Farm Guest House

Ken and Wendy Solly
15 Carter Road, York 6302
Tel: 08-9641-2183 Fax: 08-9641-1437
Email: hopefarm@yorkwa.com.au Web: www.yorkwa.com.au/HopeFarm
Cell: 0417-925-728

I chanced upon Hope Farm because the name filled me with, well... hope! Arriving unannounced – the true hospitality litmus-test – I found Wendy and Ken in the garden, seeking respite from the drubbing that their beloved Eagles were getting at the hands of my adopted footy team. Wendy bravely showed me around her home nonetheless. Airy bedrooms running off a shaded verandah have house-high brass beds wrapped in embroidered cotton sheets. The slate-floored sitting-room, which houses collections of irons and intriguing indigenous artwork, is surrounded by rat-tail latched French windows. Later, Ken led me past the swimming pool and two puffed up turkeys to introduce me to Oscar, an affectionate kangaroo with a taste for liquorice. All this in a picture-book setting: cerulean sky, luminous lawns and a whitewashed colonial mansion guarded by two pencil pine sentries overlooking the oldest inland town in WA. There's a sedate festival feel of yesteryear to York. It's the sort of place where vintage cars trundle past, jazz plays in the street and it's still considered a faux pas to win the town's cooking competition on your first outing, as Wendy discovered. I was lucky enough to sample her culinary prowess when guests arrived for tea, before being sent on my way to a chorus of cheerios, a hot buttered scone pressed into my paw. If that isn't hospitality, I don't know what is.

Rooms: 5: 3 doubles with en/s shower, one with an extra single bed, and a further 2 loft rooms sharing a bath and shower and let to a single party.
Price: $110 – $130. Single $85.
Meals: Full cooked breakfast.
Directions: Follow signs to town centre, continuing along Avon Terrace until the road forks (2km). Veer left over line and follow road to Hope Farm sign. Turn left into Carter Road.

Tardie and Yuin Stations

Jano and Michael Foulkes-Taylor
Yalgoo 6635
Tel: 08-9963-7980 Fax: 08-9963-7168
Email: tardiemob@bigpond.com.au

Tardie Station is my quintessential outback homestead. It's a six and a half hour drive from Perth and for the last three hours you rumble along well-maintained, red-earth roads on your own. The sense of wilderness and limitless space is awe-inspiring to the uninitiated. Finally you arrive at an oasis-green garden with tall trees and the old homestead hidden within. The bedrooms and bathrooms are simple and functional, but this is not why you come. Tardie offers a rich adventure that will stay with you long after the last four-star, en-suite bedroom has dissolved in your memory. You are part of the family, Jano and Michael providing hearty farm meals and fascinating conversation about life in this harsh but miraculous country. Out on the enormous farm (some 800,000 acres) there are so many special places: a disused mine, sacred Aboriginal and rock art sites, rivers and permanent waterholes for swimming, great round granite-composite boulders (like the famous Olgas) where astonishing sunsets are a reliable event. You can see for hundreds of miles if you climb to high ground. Giant red kangaroos, goannas and emus abound and the desert flowers (July – September) are a wonder of the world. Jano will draw you mud maps and send you off in your 4-wheel drive (you need to hire your own) to explore the farm. However Tardie is perfectly accessible by two-wheel-drive. I cannot recommend this experience enough.

Rooms: 2: 1 twin and 1 double sharing 1 bathroom
Price: $220 includes all meals and board. Guided tours extra.
Meals: Continental breakfast. Country-style dinners are eaten en famille using home-made produce
Directions: Ask for map to be faxed.

119

Map Number:

Northern Territory

Davidson's Camp

Philippa and Max Davidson
Arnhemland
Tel: 08-8927-5240
Email: dassafari@onaustralia.com.au Web: www.arnhemland-safaris.com
Cell: 0418-821-142

Davidson's Camp is unique in Aboriginal Arnhemland – Kakadu without the tourists and reachab
only by air, a breathtaking arrival over Mt Borradaile. On the day I visited, we drove off into th
forest in a Landrover (a group of about ten), slowly crossing streams, our guide Max (Davidso
stopping every now and again to explain the medicinal or nutritional properties of various plan
Our goal on this day was the sandstone catacombs, a rocky outcrop, beside a billabong ar
melaleuca swamp where eroding water has created a sensational labyrinth of man-sized tunne
Here we looked at cave walls and roofs daubed in natural dyes by Aboriginal artists over a fift
thousand-year period. The rock art sites reachable from the camp are numberless (and peerles
On other days you will go up to the swimming hole, half a kilometre of clear, fresh water encase
in rock with a sandy floor; or on boats out on the flood plain to bird and croc watch. As for th
lodge, you eat like kings (sashimi and barramundi the night I was there) and sleep in permane
tents with twin beds, bedside light and two standing fans. The generator goes off at about midnig
so you wake to the bird-calls of the early morning. There's a great atmosphere in the camp,
members of staff knowledgeable and enthusiastic.

Rooms: Variety of tents catering for up to 40 at the camp at any one time.
Price: 3-day package from $2,500 per person sharing. Singles $3,495. 4- and 5-day packages also available.
Meals: Everything included, except drinks.
Directions: Pick-up from wherever you are in Darwin, transfer to general aviation and flights in and out of Arnhemland included.
Postal Address: PO Box 11205, Casuarina 0811.

Indexes

Index by location

Index by house name

THE GREENWOOD GUIDE TO
SOUTH AFRICA

special hand-picked accommodation

Second Edition, 2003/4

South Africa was the first Greenwood guide and is now in its second edition. The third edition is due for publication in May 2004. The book contains B&Bs, guest houses, game lodges and farms, all of which we have personally visited and chosen for their great character and friendliness.

For more information or to order any of our guides see our web site at
www.greenwoodguides.com
or email us at
editor@greenwoodguides.com.

THE GREENWOOD GUIDE TO
NEW ZEALAND

special hand-picked accommodation

Second Edition, 2004/5

Following advanced and extremely delicate surgical procedures, we have managed to split New Zealand and Australia into two completely separate books. Both are alive and doing very well. The Greenwood Guide to New Zealand (2nd edition) contains 100 B&Bs, lodges, farms and self-catering cottages.

For more information or to order any of our guides see our web site at
www.greenwoodguides.com
or email us at
editor@greenwoodguides.com.

THE GREENWOOD GUIDE TO
CANADA

special hand-picked accommodation

First Edition

This is the latest addition to the Greenwood Guides
series. 87 great B&Bs, inns, lodges, self-catering cottages...
and even lighthouses and boats.

For more information or to order any
of our guides see our web site at
www.greenwoodguides.com
or email us at
editor@greenwoodguides.com.

Notes